Pictures That Sell

A GUIDE TO SUCCESSFUL STOCK PHOTOGRAPHY

Pictures That Sell
A GUIDE TO SUCCESSFUL STOCK PHOTOGRAPHY

COLLINS

RAY DAFFURN AND ROGER HICKS

First published 1985 by
William Collins Sons & Co Ltd.
London · Glasgow · Sydney
Auckland · Toronto · Johannesburg

Copyright © 1985
Fotobank Books Ltd.

ISBN 0 00 411720 4

Designed and produced by
Chameleon Graphic Design,
Hitchin, Hertfordshire,
England.

Production Director
Edward Kinsey

Phototypeset by
Lineage Ltd.,
Watford, England

Printed and bound by
Lee Fung Asco Printers,
Hong Kong.

Photographs supplied by
Fotobank International
Colour Library Ltd.

William Baker
Rex Bamber
Charles Bowman
Tony Burrett
Michael Busselle
Bill Carter
Stephanie Colasanti
Peter Pugh Cook
Ray Daffurn
Alex Double
John Farnham
John Flowerdew
Roger Hicks
James Holmes
Clare Hunt
JDR
John Kelly
Peter Kowal
Colin Maher
Robert Matassa
Eric Meacher
Steve Moss
Edmund Nägele
Bill Richards
Peter Rowlands
Saga/Tony Page
Frances Schultz
The English Tourist Board
Roger Tidman
Roger Weeks
Andy Williams
Robert Eames
John Robertson
Murray Irving
Michael Boys

Contents

Introduction

The role of photographic libraries, and the way in which they work, is still surprisingly little known, even to many photographers, publishers, picture users, and others who could benefit from working with a library.

This book was written by two working photographers, both of whom concentrate on stock photography, and one of whom has run a leading photographic library for almost a decade. We wrote it in response to a need: the need for answers to questions which we are asked time and time again, about what a library does, how it works, the kind of terms and conditions that are usual, what formats are best, and (again and again) what sort of photographs we have, and which pictures sell.

In fact, it goes beyond the answers to those questions. It is a manual about shooting pictures that sell, and then about selling them. We recommend that you seriously consider joining an existing library, but if you want to start your own, all the basic information you need is here; there is even a description of the computerised system of picture control which we devised at Fotobank to deal with the business side of things – and make no mistake, successful stock photographers must be good businessmen (or women) as well as good photographers. It is illustrated with over two hundred and fifty examples of stock photographs, the kind of pictures which we *know* can sell. It is not a blow-by-blow "how-to" guide (because we assume that you are already more than competent, or you would not be reading a book like this), but it does tell you how some of these successful shots were set up, and describes the circumstances in which others were discovered. We are not afraid of giving away "secrets" – there is enough work for anyone who is good enough, and who tries hard enough – and taken together, the text and the pictures form a guide which we both wish we had had when we started.

RWH
RRD
London, Bristol,
New York, Frankfurt
Paris, Los Angeles,
New Delhi, Toronto,
Venice…

Chapter 1

STOCK PHOTOGRAPHY

The Rewards of Stock Photography

The demand for photographic images in the late twentieth century is immense. Everywhere we go, we see evidence of this. Books and magazines, advertisements, travel brochures and mail-order catalogues, packaging, calendars and posters all use photographs.

These pictures have to come from somewhere, and only a fraction of them are specially shot. It is not hard to see why. It is obviously much cheaper to use a library picture of the Manhattan skyline than to commission one, and the picture library can furnish not one, but many pictures of a particular scene or subject. The client can pick from a whole range of shots, taken at different times of day or night, different seasons, different weather conditions, different angles, to be sure of getting exactly what he wants – and the pictures are available immediately.

Picture libraries have to get their pictures from somewhere and they have to keep their stocks comprehensive and up-to-date. Very few of the largest libraries rely mainly, or entirely, on paid staff photographers, but the vast majority rely on freelances. As long as the photographer continues to supply them with saleable pictures, they do not care particularly whether he is an established professional, a struggling assistant or an amateur. It is quality, and a reasonably constant flow of pictures, that are important.

There are some photographers who earn a substantial income solely from stock photography, but for most professionals and amateurs alike it is a means of earning income from existing assets in a way that is enjoyable in itself. The picture buyer rarely knows or cares

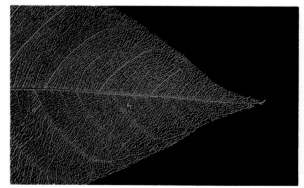

Pictures of young, attractive couples always sell well; a picture like this could be used for almost anything. The picture of the leaf is more specialised, but it is a dramatic image which could be used as a background for text or for a composite picture; it symbolises decay, autumn, delicacy, and fragility.

There is always a demand for food shots, for cookery, travel, and many other markets. They are not always easy to set up – but they can be very profitable.

who took the photograph that he uses, because it has no effect on the price that he pays for the right picture. There are, of course, exceptions and sometimes the photographer's name will help to sell the picture: Sam Haskins and Michael Boys can command a premium over, say, Fred Bloggs. In other words, pictures usually sell solely on their own merits, unlike most 'semi-professional' fields of photography where the amateur succeeds by setting his prices very low.

For the professional, the advantages are clear. Often, stock photography can ride on the back of other work: for example, a commissioned glamour shoot in an exotic location with two or three models can cost a fortune, but extending it for two or three days at the photographer's expense, or taking a stopover on the way home, is relatively inexpensive and can earn many times the outlay involved. It is also a good excuse for staying on a shoot for a few days longer; most photographers enjoy their work and even if the extra time is partly holiday it is still tax-deductible.

By their very nature, panoramic shots are eye-catching; but it is not always easy to ensure a balanced composition. Paradoxically, this is not necessarily a disadvantage in stock photography, where there often has to be room for text.

Another picture with plenty of room for text. The composition, as a picture, is not particularly exciting; but the contrast of the colours is dramatic and eye-catching, which can be equally important.

For the amateur, there is not only the income itself, but the added advantage that all relevant expenditure can be set against income for tax purposes (it is not worth trying to conceal the income from the Inland Revenue). As a bonus, it also gives some direction to the amateur's photography; with no goal in mind, the hobby can seem rather futile. It could be said that competitions also provide a goal, but stock photography is usually more profitable and has the advantage that the photographer is dealing with real buyers in the real world rather than with an arbitrarily band of judges who are often as much in touch with the real world as most of the pictures they judge. Of course selling stock pictures is not just a matter of pulling a few pictures out of your files, sending them to a library, and then waiting for the money to roll in; if it were, there would not be much need for this book. Instead, you have to plan what you are doing, learn what sort of pictures sell and what

sort do not, and submit the right pictures, in the right way, to the right picture library. It may be that you want to set up your own picture library (also covered in this book), but even at this stage it is worth a warning that running a successful picture library can be a full-time job.

At the outset, the most important things to emphasise are quality and quantity. Make no mistake, the pictures that you submit to the library must be technically superb. This means that all originals must be on correctly exposed transparency material, though in some cases (for example, where there is a subtle grain pattern) it may be a good idea to make prints for the client, to aid selection. You must also pay attention to detail: a dropped cigarette packet in the foreground can completely destroy the saleability of a scenic shot for most purposes. There is a market for black and white pictures too, though expenses tend to be higher and income lower, so monochrome is hardly touched on in this book.

The Eiffel Tower could scarcely be a more photographed subject, but by using it as a background to another equally typical Parisian subject, the cherub-supported lamps, a truly romantic ambiance is created. The spectral starburst filter adds another touch of magic – an example where the use of a 'trick' filter is more than justified.

As for quantity, you should be able to feed the library at least a hundred pictures a year, and preferably several hundreds or even thousands. From the library's point of view, this is a matter of simple accounting: it is easier to deal with ten photographers, each of whom has a thousand pictures in the library, than with a thousand photographers with ten pictures each. From the photographer's point of view, it means building up a stock of many thousands of first-class pictures, which obviously increases earning potential. It also encourages the library to take your work seriously – if they value your submissions, they will want to work as closely as possible with you, make suggestions about how to improve your sales, and possibly even pass on commissions.

Different photographers and different libraries have different approaches, specialities, contacts, marketing experience, concerns, and so on, and it is important to match the two carefully. The authors of this book are photographers, and both are involved in the running of a major picture library, so it is written from both sides of the fence. The vast majority of the pictures here were taken from picture libraries. We hope that when you have finished reading the book you will say, 'I could go out and do that!', and then go right ahead and do it.

Children of any culture are always appealing, and when they are made up like this and wearing traditional clothes, the effect is multiplied. For editorial use, an extensive caption would be required, but where the picture is used to create a mood, it tells its own story.

Pictures of two girls together can be difficult to achieve tastefully, but here the overall effect is open, natural, and suitable even for the more liberal general-interest magazines.

Chapter 2

THE PHOTO LIBRARY

Reproduction Rights

A photo library sells the right to reproduce a given picture in a certain way at a certain time. In order to understand how this works it is necessary to have some understanding of copyright – literally, the right to control the making of copies.

There are two systems of copyright law. In most countries copyright automatically belongs to the photographer, unless the photograph is commissioned, in which case the copyright belongs to the person who commissioned the picture. There are, however, many local variations on this. In England, for example, the 1956

Potentially useful as a poster, a postcard, or a backdrop to an advertisement, this picture illustrates how different buyers might purchase different rights in the same picture, without ever encroaching upon one another's sales.

Copyright Act provides that it is the owner of the sensitive material on which the photograph is originally taken who owns the copyright, unless the photographer takes the picture in the course of his employment by a newspaper or magazine proprietor, when the proprietor has the first right to publish, after which the copyright reverts to the photographer.

The other system, which obtains in the United States, is that the photographer must register his work, image by image, for full copyright protection. It is possible to register groups of images, either by re-photographing

This picture is very awarkedly composed for, say, a jigsaw; but an advertiser might find the foliage and path on the left ideal for inserting copy, and another user might decide to crop the picture to suit his purposes.

them on a single sheet of film, or by binding them together in a single book or booklet, but otherwise a stiff fee is payable for each photograph. This is obviously expensive and time-consuming, but the 1976 Copyright Act seems to have been drafted with very little concern for this.

There are many other technicalities, such as the meaning of the word 'publication'. Legally, this usually means 'made available for public viewing' and not (as many people think) 'reproduced in a book, magazine, etc.' The period of copyright also varies: it may be for 50 years after the taking of the picture, for 50 years after the publication of the picture, or for 50 years after the death of the photographer. In the United States the position also depends on whether the pictures were taken before or after 1978. It is clearly impossible to give a full guide to copyright law here, but the photographer must be aware of the problems.

The copyright holder may however assign or sell his copyright and, even if the photographer was commissioned to take the pictures, he may still reserve copyright. Copyright is not normally assigned to the library, which means that it cannot be sold without the express permission of the photographer. In fact, the library usually tries to limit reproduction rights as far as possible in order to preserve other rights for future sales. Reproduction rights will usually be limited geographically for a certain language, with the price depending on the area covered, and they may be exclusive or non-exclusive. Exclusive rights are usually limited in time (i.e. for one year, or for up to five years), and by market (such as 'travel brochure use' or 'postcard'). They may be licensed for a single use, in a particular advertisement for example, or they may be licensed for a number of different uses – advertising in magazines, on posters, and on packaging perhaps. Typically, the library's delivery note will list the terms of the licence; see Appendix 1 for an example.

Primarily an editorial picture, shot for a particular story, an image like this is still worth keeping in the library in case a request does come up.

13

Photographers and Libraries

For most photographers it is not a difficult choice between running their own library and putting their pictures with an established one. Running a library as a one-man show does mean that you remain in control of your pictures and that you have a strong incentive to sell them. It also means that you keep all the income yourself. Against this, you cannot take pictures while you are administering the library, and administration is unlikely to be as enjoyable as photography and requires different skills. Even if you run the library single-handed there will be overheads, and if you hire anyone else these will be even higher. In any case, an established picture library can probably get a better price and sell to a wider market, to say nothing of knowing the ins and outs of contracts and having much more clout when it comes to dealing with awkward customers. Those who want to run their own library are referred to Appendix 2 for more detailed information. In the body of this book, we are concerned more with illustrating the broad outlines of running a library, and with photographers who want to sell their pictures through established libraries.

For the photographer, finding the right library is not easy. Firstly, they must handle your sort of work; secondly they must be reliable; and thirdly they must offer reasonable terms and conditions. In addition to these considerations you must be able to establish a good working relationship.

Reliability is probably the easiest question to settle, by asking both photographers and picture users. Most photo libraries are honest and those that are not soon acquire a well-deserved bad reputation. Some sell better than others and this soon becomes clear after a little research, though you have to make some allowance for the fact that no photographer ever believes that his library is selling his pictures as well as it should.

The other points can only be settled by going round and meeting the personnel, but be sure to write or telephone first to make sure that you are not wasting either their time or yours. The working relationship is more important to some people than others, but in any creative field such as this one it is obviously a major drawback if you do not get on with the people involved. The only major area of contention is likely to be about what constitutes 'reasonable' terms and conditions.

To begin with, the usual split on picture fees is 50 per cent to the photographer, 50 per cent to the library. At first sight this may seem excessive, but when you look at the library's overheads and allow for the fact that they are doing all the marketing, selling and accounting, it does not look quite so bad. Just try working out what it would cost you to achieve the same level of sales – assuming you could. In any case, it is the standard deal, so there is not much you can do unless you are already so well-known that you can negotiate a more advantageous split.

You will also be asked to sign an exclusive contract, usually for a minimum period of three or even five years, and to accept that it may take up to three months (six in some contracts) to get your pictures back. Once again, although this looks fairly stiff, there are good reasons. Exclusivity is necessary in order to safeguard the client, the photographer, and the library. If other similar pictures are available elsewhere, the client will not be assured that he is getting exclusive rights. The photographer may not be able to prove who sold his picture, which leaves him unable to extract payment from the appropriate source, and the library can lose both income and credibility. The minimum period is necessary because experience has shown that a

Colourful local characters are always worth recording, especially when (as here) they sum up the spirit of a place. Bear in mind that with increased travel, pictures such as these can no longer sell on novelty value alone; the client who requests such a picture probably has half a dozen or a dozen to select from.

Sports such as canoeing are often featured in all sorts of magazines, and good pictures are hard to come by. Often, a photographer who successfully specialises in a sport will be an enthusiast himself.

photographer's pictures may hardly sell at all in the first year after he joins the library, and that sales are rarely very good in the second year; it is the third and subsequent years when they really begin to sell well. The three or five year minimum therefore ensures that the library gets a reasonable return for its efforts, and that the photographer does not withdraw in disgust and blacken their name when initial sales are not as good as he had hoped. No-one is sure why there is this 'incubation period', but all libraries agree that it exists. Finally, the three or six month period for withdrawing pictures simply reflects reality: if the pictures are with a client, it can take this long to get them back, and no library is going to jeopardise its own standing by trying to get them back in a hurry. A typical photographer's contract, from Fotobank International, is given in Appendix 1.

As for the library wanting your pictures — this whole book is about just that. It deals with the principal markets, with the kind of pictures that sell, and so on, until in Chapter 10 it tells you how to prepare a submission.

This picture might suit certain types of editorial use perfectly, or it might be combined with a picture of the tractor driver and his family at dinner. It is not, however, a particularly readily saleable picture, and many people might find it rather murky and dull. You should also ask yourself carefully whether the 'trick' filter really adds anything, or merely makes a dull sky still more tiresome.

Fotobank has an extensive collection of pictures concerning wine – a subject dear to the authors' hearts – and a dramatic picture like this one goes far beyond a merely editorial shot, although it was originally taken for this purpose.

On the library's side the problems are no less complex. To begin with, there is the question of personality, just as there is for the photographer; but there is also the question of guessing the direction which the photographer's work is going to take. Only rarely does a photographer come to a library with a clear idea of what sort of photographs sell, and it can take a year or more before he (or she) learns what the library can and cannot sell; this is one of the reasons for the 'incubation period' already mentioned, and also accounts for the way in which later submissions often sell better than earlier ones, which is something that many photographers find hard to understand. If the photographer and the library understand one another, then both can work towards saleability; but if there is conflict, which is by no means impossible, the library can invest a lot of time and mental strain in dealing with a photographer whose work turns out never to be really saleable anyway.

Spotting photographers is not easy, and many libraries approach the problem from two directions at once. Usually, there are plenty of photographers who want to show portfolios of their work, and this is one obvious source. But often, there are photographers with potential who may go to other libraries unless you can get them first, and this is why some libraries have a policy of taking amateur magazines and going to minor exhibitions whenever possible, so that they can spot potentially successful stock photographers and approach them before anyone else has a chance.

Once the photographer has been taken on to the books, there is also the problem of the 'prima donna' who is never satisfied with his (or her) sales, and who constantly telephones or even calls in to ask why the library has not sold more of his pictures. There are also photo-

graphers who have some difficulty in understanding what exclusivity means, and who place their pictures with other libraries, or sell them themselves; there are those who do not bother to edit their pictures properly; there are the ones whose captions are either terse to the point of useless, or actually wrong; there are the ones who want to treat the library as a correspondence course in photography, and who want to know in detail just why this picture has been accepted and this one rejected…the possibilities are endless. Tact and politeness can only go so far with some people: there has to come a point where you tell them what they are doing wrong, and leave it at that. But this is where the 5-year contract can work to the library's disadvantage: the photographer may be prepared to complain on a regular basis, but not to make the effort to remove his pictures and go elsewhere. This is, of course, one of the reasons for being suspicious when a photographer changes libraries, and for talking to the old library whenever possible. It is, of course, foolish to be too suspicious; but it is also foolish not to be careful.

As a picture, the composition of this Las Vegas scene leaves a lot to be desired; but as a stock shot, with plenty of room for text and almost a montage of the well-known downtown casinos, it is excellent. Incidentally, notice the way in which flare has destroyed the ultimate sharpness of this picture; a contrastier lens would have given a picture with even more impact. This is where 'straight' wide-angles score over the reverse-telephoto designs which have to be used on reflexes.

Cataloguing

A client may contact half a dozen libraries for pictures, specifying the subjects he wants and the intended use of the pictures. After selecting the pictures he wants he will return the others to the libraries they came from.

This may sound straightforward enough, but it has several consequences which are less immediately obvious. Firstly, the pictures must be accurately captioned, or the picture library may not be able to select appropriate pictures. Secondly, they must be catalogued in such a way that finding them (and returning them to the right place) is quick and easy. Thirdly, they must bear the library's name, so that the customer knows where they came from. Fourthly, they must bear the photographer's name (or a library code indicating this) so that the library knows whose they are. And fifthly, if there are any restrictions on the sale of the picture, these must be made clear with a note such as 'Not to be used for UK travel market' or 'American postcard rights sold for 1 year 2/12/85'. These notes are sometimes made in code, so that prospective customers are not put off by the knowledge that the picture has been used before. Obviously, if there is any likelihood of conflict the pictures will not be sent out, and if the client changes his mind about the prospective use he will be advised of any such possibility.

Captions are primarily the responsibility of the photographer; the caption slip will normally be pre-printed with the library's name, and the photographer's name (or code) will be added as a matter of course. Restrictions can be noted as necessary when the picture is sold and periodically updated.

Cataloguing is, however, a much more awkward task: to begin with, you need to devise a hierarchical filing system. Some libraries use the international Dewey decimal system, but as this was designed for printed books its shortcomings are considerable. Otherwise, each library uses its own system with three or four levels of heading. For example, the main heading 'United States' might have a sub-division by states, a second sub-division by cities or countries, and a third sub-division describing the actual subject of the picture.

No matter what system you use, the difficulty is clear. Consider, for example, the caption: 'United States: Arizona: sunset over desert cactus'. It is admirably clear, but do you classify it under Arizona, sunset, desert or cactus? The only real option is cross-referencing: file it under any of those headings, but make sure that anyone searching under the others will also be referred to that one. This is where computerized cataloguing is ideal, as a keyword search can locate almost any subject very quickly indeed and indicate where to find the actual pictures.

A picture such as this could be catalogued according to location, but would this tell you very much? The fact that it is a lace stall is surely more important, and the soft-focus effect is also worth mentioning in cross-referencing; it could be very useful if a client specifically demanded something with a nostalgic mood.

Below
Once again, the precise location is likely to be less important than the mood; but you have to put the picture somewhere...

Dealing in Pictures

The ideal picture library, from the picture researcher's point of view, has a wide range of pictures of the sort that he wants; can find and deliver those pictures quickly and easily; and is readily accessible. Within reason, price is a secondary consideration, because it is a matter for negotiation anyway and because the lowest prices in the world are no use unless the library has the pictures that he wants.

From the library's point of view, it is important to send out only the pictures that the customer wants; to ensure that they are out for as little time as possible; to ensure that they are safely returned; to get the best price possible; and to get the money in as fast as possible.

Even the first point, the range of pictures, is more complicated than it sounds. Different libraries have different strengths, and picture researchers are aware of this. For certain pictures, they will go to specialist libraries, or to libraries which have specialist collections; often, the specialist libraries actually offer less choice than the specialist collections in larger general libraries. For example, the specialist collections at Fotobank International include subjects as diverse as food, underwater pictures, and Tibetans in exile. For more general pictures, clients will either go to the library that they know best, or ask several libraries who are known for their wide-ranging collections.

It is therefore important for people to have a clear image of the strengths and resources of a particular library, and this is where marketing is important. A library which pretends to have everything, but never delivers, will rapidly acquire a bad reputation; on the other hand, unless the library constantly makes the customer aware of what it has got, it may be missing valuable sales opportunities. A point which is less immediately obvious is that the pictures which are on offer must be at least as good as anything that other libraries have: if 'make-weights' are sent out, it is merely another version of promising what cannot be delivered.

It is important to distinguish between the brochure, which is primarily pictorial, and the catalogue, which consists of subject headings and may contain no pictures at all. A brochure should contain a good cross-section of the library's pictures, possibly in categories for ease of reference, and must be well printed; a bad brochure is worse than no brochure at all. Some libraries use posters instead of (or as well as) brochures; but whether posters or brochures are used, they should not stand alone nor be allowed to stand for too long. At least once a year, and preferably half-yearly or quarterly, the library should remind past and possible customers that it still exists, and tell them about any additions to the range of subjects covered, or other infor-

This is certainly a picture of a castle – but if the client had Schloss Neuschwanstein in mind, it may well be useless. This is why it is so essential to try to determine the clients' needs as accurately as possible.

A perennial seller, and a picture which had to be carefully set up. It is simply not possible to wait for pictures like this to come along, but they can repay the cost of staging them many times over.

If you have any aerial pictures (or 'mock aerials', shot from high buildings) it is always worth including them in your brochure; they are always in demand, and frequently hard to find.

mation about how the library's facilities have been improved. The reminder need not even be in colour (though it will help if it is); it is usually very effective to present it as a newsletter. The brochure itself should be updated every two or three years, both as a precaution against becoming dated and to present new pictures: a surprising number of customers will order pictures that they see in the brochure, and this can offset the cost of reprinting to quite an extent.

Various other forms of advertising should also be considered, such as the annual trade publications aimed at advertising agencies, designers, and photographers; specialist journals (who may also be prepared to do feature articles); and direct mailing. You can even turn advertisements for new staff to advantage; by phrasing them carefully you can make sure that they will be read by anyone who sees them,

Pictures of girls are one of the staples of stock photography, and some examples should always be included in the brochure.

Details do not generally sell as well as more general shots, but when you are there, they cost very little extra to shoot and can be invaluable when the client needs more than one picture of a particular scene.

which helps to keep your name in the public eye – or at least, in the eye of the people who matter.

It is extremely important to plan all advertising carefully: analysis of the past years' sales can tell you when it is best to promote the various aspects of your business, to whom you ought to send your direct mail shots, and so forth. At Fotobank, our computer system (see Appendix 2) provides us with analyses of sales by subject, by time of year, and by client (and the clients' specialities). This enables us to make very accurate and specific mailing shots, which we have found are much more cost-effective than mass mailings; but without the computer, it would probably be more cost effective to use a mailing company and a commercial mailing list, because the time, expense and trouble of preparing your own mail shots can be excessive.

You can also use international fairs as a valuable means of promoting yourself (and checking out the competition!); some libraries arrange deals with publishers at these, offering a reduced rate across the year in return for an exclusive contract, or at least a guaranteed minimum annual sale.

Monochromatic colour is always moody, and can show the range of work which the library offers.

These two pictures have two things in common. They are both lit from the right, and they both come from the same library. In England, it might seem that one was exotic and the other commonplace – but in (for example) New York, the mask might be obtainable from a museum, while the cricketer was the really difficult shot.

One last point about marketing concerns overseas sales. Although it might seem attractive to send out a multilingual brochure, this is never as effective as being in the country itself, or as having a good agent. Although the agent usually takes 40% of the picture fee, he will normally be better placed to judge the market, and many difficulties with language, local law, and so forth are avoided. Whether you are dealing direct or through an agent, a private Telex or cable is virtually indispensable, for speed, cost-effectiveness, and because it solves many of the problems of time differences between different areas. It also provides you with a clear written record in case of dispute!

Finding the pictures is a matter of internal organisation, but delivery is another matter. This is where accessibility is important. Ideally, most picture researchers like to go to the library themselves, so that they can go through the maximum possible number of pictures and pick the ones they want. Anyone who has ever done any picture research will be familiar with three advantages to this. First, they do not have to rely on the library's interpretation of their written instructions. Secondly, there is always the possibility of finding a picture which is actually better than the one which they had in mind, but which would not have been covered by a written brief. And thirdly, even if they do not always have time to go along in person, they can build up a personal relationship with the people at the library, so that the library's picture editor is better able to gauge their needs and to interpret their requests. This is particularly important if the brief is not particularly clear; the staff at the picture library must know which questions to ask in order to ensure that the client gets the sort of pictures he wants.

If the premises are likely to be visited by customers, they must be reasonably attractive and convenient. There is no great need to be in the most fashionable part of town, but the surroundings should not be too sleazy either. An essential requirement inside the library itself is plenty of light boxes, which should be colour matched for critical picture selection, though there may also be non-colour-matched boxes (or panels or tables) for quick selection from the files or for sorting large numbers of pictures. At Fotobank, we have a bank of non-colour-matched panels above the files on the non-window side of the room for checking; on the other side, window light is sufficient. Two other desirable features are non-illuminated tables or work surfaces beside the light boxes, which makes taking and reading notes much easier, and a comfortable seating area away from the picture files where customers can sit and have a drink, and talk about their requirements. This

Skies are steady sellers in stock photography, usually for backgrounds, and soft, romantic pictures such as this carefully posed shipboard scene are another staple.

should be the only place where coffee is allowed! If chilled drinks (fruit juice and Perrier water) are also available, so much the better.

Although there are still some libraries who use a 'shoe-box' system of picture storage, more and more are going over to suspended files in standard filing cabinets. The advantages are considerable: space is used to very good advantage, several pictures can be examined at once (instead of pulling out each picture individually), the cabinets afford good physical protection (especially the fireproof variety), and re-filing is much easier than with the shoe-box system.

The location of the library can also be important if the pictures are wanted urgently – and all advertising agencies want everything now, if not yesterday. If the library is in the same city as the customer, it can send the pictures round by cab, or by motorcycle messenger, though if motorcycle couriers are used, it is essential to pack the pictures very carefully indeed: rain, or the rider falling off, are only the more obvious hazards. Of course, if speed is not of the

One of the advantages to the client in using stock, rather than commissioned, photography is that he can choose from all the seasons of the year and the times of the day – immediately.

essence, or if the customer is too far away to use a courier, the mails will have to be used. Once again, careful packing is essential, and the service used should be chosen carefully. In most countries, there is a choice of letter or parcel post, and there may be different classes (= speeds) of letter post, express delivery options, insurance, and so forth. There are also various kinds of special delivery by other carriers, so speed, cost, convenience and security (including the scale of compensation in case of loss) should all be considered together.

When the client comes in himself, he will usually want to see as many pictures as possible, but if he requests pictures to be sent, they should be carefully selected, for two good reasons. The first is that he is probably busy (otherwise he would have come in himself), and he is therefore relying on the library to do his preliminary selection for him. The second is that pictures which are with one customer cannot be sent to another, so if another request for the same sort of picture comes in, and duplicates are not available, the library suffers the double disadvantage of not being able to supply the picture (which may mean that the customer goes

Morning by the riverside, early summer flowers: stock pictures are available "off the shelf" at any time of year, and without danger of a washout or a reshoot.

'Character' studies of people are always in demand, but the people must be smart, healthy, and happy looking.

elsewhere next time) and of losing potential income.

At Fotobank, our immediate response to an enquiry is to reach for one of our standard enquiry forms, which prompts our librarians to check all the necessary information for selecting and sending a picture or pictures to the client. If we have pictures which the client wants, we make an appropriate selection in keeping with his wishes, and log the despatch on to our computer system: picture details, date of despatch, and so forth. At the end of the month, holdings are checked by the computer, and the status of each set of pictures determined: returned, held for selection, no further response, or whatever. If there has been no response, the computer system sends out a progressive series of automatic reminders, including information about holding fees payable if pictures are not returned by the due date.

The holding fee must be set high enough to be a strong incentive for the customer to return the pictures, but not so high that it acts as a deterrent. If it is too high, the customer may decide not to use the library in future, or he may simply decide not to pay. In theory, the money would be recoverable through the courts; in practice, the trouble this causes, and the ill-will it generates, means that this is not always a real option. A similar problem arises with lost or damaged transparencies. Most libraries specify a fairly punitive sum for lost pictures – at the time of writing, usually between $250 and $1,000 – but they also recognise that they may not be able to recover the money, and therefore specify in their contracts with photographers that they will not be liable. Insurance is alarmingly expensive, and should normally only be considered if the pictures are outstanding and the photographer is threatening to leave unless they are insured; even then, he would be expected to pay 50% of the cost of insurance – which may persuade him that he didn't really want the pictures insured anyway...

Getting the best price possible for the rights which are sold is a matter for experience and diplomacy. Only experience will tell what the market will bear, which is the only factor determining prices, and experience and diplomacy together are needed to know how to temper that price. The highest price this time may mean no sale next time, because the customer goes elsewhere, and it may sometimes be better to accept an unusually low price rather than losing the business altogether – though if this is done too often, it can lead to the library acquiring a reputation for low prices, which will prejudice the chances of getting good prices next time. It is also very important to agree the nature of the rights which are being sold, for the client as well as for the library; after all, by buying only those rights which he needs, and no more, the client saves a considerable amount of money, especially when compared with the cost of a commissioned shoot.

A useful winemaking shot: the versatility is increased by the fact that it was shot in England.

Many libraries now make a flat handling charge for all picture requests, though this may be reduced or even waived for regular clients if they call in several times in connection with a particular project. It is normally a fairly small fee, designed to cover the actual administrative costs of selecting pictures, and to act as a deterrent to those picture editors who send for pictures from a dozen libraries every time they need a photograph. It also covers the 'unofficial' uses which are sometimes made of pictures, where (for example) an advertising agency has a print made of a picture without telling the library, uses it in a layout, and then does not

subsequently use it commercially – the 'X-Acto knife art director' is a well-known figure. Although some clients object to handling fees, it is interesting that they are usually the worst offenders, and the most likely to try to use the picture for a presentation without telling the library. Unless the fee is unreasonably high, most accept it as fair: normally, the library should ascertain at the outset whether the picture is to be used for presentations or layouts, so that a fair fee can be agreed beforehand. Negotiations after the event are usually much more difficult!

Finally, the importance of knowing the exact whereabouts and status of every picture at all times cannot be overemphasised. The most efficient way of doing this is probably with a computer, so that the whole business is fully integrated. When the pictures are sent out, they are logged on the computer; at the end of twenty eight days, the computer prints out a reminder that the pictures should have been returned; when they are returned, they are logged in; any use is noted; and bills are produced, with reminders. Then, when the money is paid, the photographer's account can be credited, and the money due will appear on the monthly or quarterly statement. A summary of the Fotobank system (for which the software is commercially available) appears in Appendix 2.

Chapter 3

PICTURES THAT SELL

Introduction

Stock pictures are normally required to do one of two things. One is to sum up a particular subject, and the other is to convey or create a particular mood. They are almost invariably required to illustrate something which already exists – a book, an advertising concept, or whatever. This generally means that experimental pictures, or pictures that do not immediately make themselves clear, will not be as well received as more straightforward images. In fact, if you ask most picture researchers, picture editors, and library owners what they are really after they will often tell you, 'The same old clichés – in a new form.'

Just occasionally, an apparently 'uncommercial' picture will catch the attention of a particular client, and when it does, it may command a surprisingly high fee; but this is so much a matter of luck, and of one individual's taste, that it is never worth relying on. On the other hand, there will always be a tourist-brochure market for pictures of pretty girls in swimsuits, or of couples wandering hand in hand through some romantic location, or pictures that convey the mystery of the East, or show the vastness of the Grand Canyon. Even old clichés, such as kittens peering winsomely from baskets of knitting, continue to sell. All these subjects have been photographed a million times: the successful stock picture shows them as if we were seeing them for the first time.

It is not difficult to see why these pictures are always in demand. More often than not, stock pictures used to foster an existing illusion, or reinforce an existing image, rather than to say anything new. We all have an image of, say, the Kasbah; and someone who is selling holidays in Morocco wants a picture which reinforces that image and makes us want to go there. 'Slice of life' realism may make striking pictures, but apart from editorial use, and photographic books and magazines, the market is very limited.

After the content, the second requirement is that the pictures should be up-to-date, or at least that they should not be obviously dated. Clothes, cars, even buildings change: this is another reason why there is an insatiable demand for the same old favourites, over and over again.

Thirdly, detail is important. Cluttered backgrounds, expressions on faces, poses: all of these make the difference between an excellent picture and one that is merely competent. Of course, technical quality is taken for granted.

Finally, the compositional requirements for stock shots are not always the same as for other types of photography. For example, many art directors will be looking for a picture which can be cropped to fit the space available, and if composition and framing are too tight, they will turn a picture down. On the other hand, a properly composed and framed picture will always be more eye-catching and visually satisfying than one with no real shape or form, so this is a difficult tight-rope to walk! Again, if text is to be dropped into the picture, a convenient blank space is desirable: sky and sea, or sand, are old favourites. Without the text the picture might appear unbalanced, but then a conventional composition might leave no room for text.

You can almost smell the clear air and feel this chill in this evocative image. It could be from many parts of the world; the mood is more important than the precise location. On the other hand, captions must be accurate, because there is always at least one reader who recognises a mis-captioned scene and writes in to complain! This can be very embarrassing for the picture editor, the photo library, and everyone else concerned, and does nothing to enhance the photographer's reputation.

This is an unusual picture, in that almost everyone who sees it is sure that they know where it was taken – but the location has been identified as Mexico, Peru, the Dominican Republic, and even Portugal. The old man with the bird, obviously in a market place (you can see the out-of-focus stall behind) is a timeless image. The original Kodacrhome was very slightly cropped in order to 'lose' as much as possible of the man on the right.

The Market

It is more accurate to speak of 'markets' for stock pictures, rather than 'the market'. The needs of each buyer are different, and the pictures must be tailored to those needs or they will not sell. The market can be divided into four areas: promotional, editorial, visual, and filler.

Promotional pictures are not just those used on advertising billboards, or in magazines and travel brochures; they are also widely used in packaging. The obvious and glamorous example is a record sleeve (which is one of the few markets for a genuinely experimental or creative shot), but if you look around you will see all sorts of boxes, bottles, packets and cans that are illustrated. Some are clearly specially shot, but others are equally clearly not.

Editorial pictures rarely command such high prices as promotional ones, but they may be more satisfying and interesting to take and, because publishers tend to take larger numbers of pictures than advertising and promotional users, lower fees are offset by increased num-

bers of sales, so it is not a field to be dismissed. 'Editorial use' covers a wide range of markets, from books and magazines to audio-visual productions and even television, and there may well be pictures which can be used editorially as well as promotionally. With travel pictures, in particular, it may be hard to distinguish between editorial and promotional use, especially in a magazine issue devoted to holidays. Editorial pictures need not, however, be so relentlessly up-beat as promotional ones. In the editorial world, it does rain. Not everyone strides confidently forward, and there is generally more scope for showing the world as it is, rather than as we (or our advertising agencies) would like to see it.

The third category, the visual, may seem odd: surely all pictures are visual? Well yes, but what we mean here is the kind of picture which can be relied upon, without any help from the text, to create an impression. They are sometimes known as 'one page stoppers', and

This picture has sold consistently for a considerable time, because it is not only an attractive composition; it can also be cropped in a number of ways to emphasise the agricultural aspect, the father and son taking the dog for a walk, or the misty hills in the background. Or, of course, it can be printed 'all in' to give a timeless picture of the English countryside as it is firmly fixed in everyone's dreams.

A slow exposure, necessary for the small stop which this picture required for depth of field, has given an ethereal and magical feeling to the flowing water.
To anyone who knows Paris, the image is unforgettable; to anyone who does not, it must surely inspire a desire to go to the city of lovers, of cobbled streets, and of Toulouse Lautrec.

although the purest form might be the poster, which is basically a reproduction of a photograph sold on its own merits, such pictures are also used on book and magazine front covers, on calendars, on greetings cards, and even in men's magazines, though the last is a somewhat specialised use and is covered at greater length in Chapter 7.

The last category, the filler, is self explanatory. Magazine editors in particular know that too much text looks dull, and that it is likely to be skipped by most people, and so they use pictures to break it up. A filler picture may be loosely related to the text or it may stand alone. As likely as not, it will come out of the magazine's own files because it will be needed at short notice, and cheaply. This is the market that so many of the old 'How To Make Money From Your Camera' books covered, but it pays so poorly that it is not mentioned again here; it is very much the poor relation of the other three markets.

The caption for this picture reads, "India: grain harvesting near Agra, Uttar Pradesh". Detailed captions, with all relevant facts, are essential for this sort of picture, which will be used editorially more often than in advertising, etc. Although pictures like this would normally be shot on 35mm, note how the use of the 6 x 7cm format has given improved sharpness, especially in the grain. The larger format also stands out from 35mm pictures when they are presented together.

Promotional Pictures

Many advertising pictures are specially shot (for obvious reasons), but there are still many campaigns in which some or all of the pictures come from libraries. Even major campaigns may require library pictures to combine with text or to montage with other pictures, and in lower-budget campaigns the funds may not stretch to specially-shot material.

In either case, the picture is not usually required to show the product itself. This suits the photographer as he does not want to show a specific product in stock pictures for fear that it will prejudice sales to other manufacturers and their agencies. Often, there is no immediate or obvious link to the product at all – the picture is used to create a mood or demonstrate a contrast, or the link is made by copy or artwork.

In packaging, the picture may be more closely related to the subject. For example, there are innumerable brands of pet food. Even major brands may use stock pictures because of the difficulty of shooting good pictures to order, and the lesser brands (especially supermarket own brand labels) will almost certainly use a stock shot, if they use photography at all. A typical picture would be of a cat or dog tucking into a bowl of food, though they might also use a cat yawning or washing, or a dog licking its lips and looking as if it was expecting to be fed. Often the animal is required to look up, so that it appears to be looking at the brand name at the top of the package.

Pictures in travel brochures, car hire brochures or any other form of advertising brochure, are somewhere between these two approaches. The pictures must be consistent

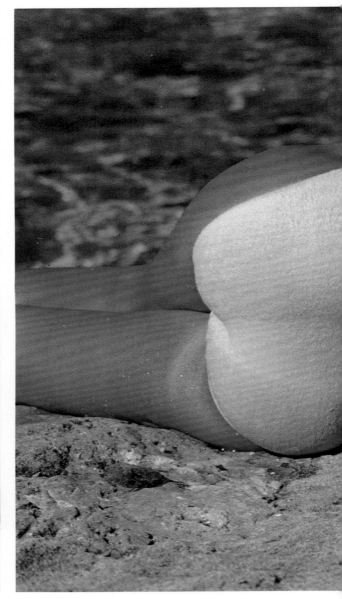

A cat licking its lips; a universal symbol of contentment and expectation combined, and one which is (comparatively) easily achieved by smearing a little bacon fat on the feline's whiskers.

with the life-style promised, and reasonably relevant, but not necessarily literal. Thus a holiday brochure for Morocco might concentrate on the hotels, and show people beside the pool; but it might also show a traditional *souk* or market, not with the intention of attracting Moroccan stall-holders, but because people on holiday there can expect to see exotic sights.

The hotels, incidentally, are often specially shot, but at least one library has a profitable policy of always photographing the local hotels when on location in the popular holiday destinations. They then sell the reproduction rights to travel companies, who are delighted because it saves them the trouble, expense, and risk of commissioning a special shoot.

Pictures of pretty girls are always in demand, and a modest, natural-looking picture like this one could be used to advertise sun-tan oil, holidays, make-up, or many other products, as well as lending itself to editorial use for travel, physical fitness, dieting, or whatever.

An apparently spontaneous picture like this is almost impossible to come by accidentally, even if you live in Palos Verdes. Professional models, or friends who look the part, almost invariably have to be used. They can be asked to run past the same spot again and again, together or separately, in a number of different ways.

In any sort of promotional picture, the whole emphasis must be up-beat. Usually the sky will be blue, the people will be happy, smiling, fit and healthy; the streets will be clean; there will be no rusty, clapped-out local taxis in shot, no beggars and no dead dogs. The whole

A picture such as this one, on the other hand, is almost impossible to pose. As is clear from the compressed perspective and shallow depth of field, a long-focus lens was used to obtain this picture, part of a series showing Chelsea pensioners.

scene, in fact, will have been sanitised and idealised. Regardless of what you think of this, the simple fact is that it is what sells; if you want to photograph blind beggars and crippled children, do not expect to sell to this market. And if you cannot get the right kind of picture – because of the weather, because the hotel is covered in scaffolding, or because you cannot get the right people into shot and the wrong people out of shot – then save your film. It is tempting to shoot what you can just because you are there, but there is no point because the pictures will not sell anyway.

Even the kind of picture that might seem ideal for a 'Get Away From It All' campaign, with someone huddling in a doorway against torrential rain, is rarely possible if the weather is wrong. For every person who looks attractively windswept, or even smilingly rained upon, there are a hundred who look drenched and miserable. In any case, a campaign which is that subtle is likely to be specially shot, so that the same person can be shown in the next picture, magically transported to the Caribbean or wherever.

The best way to understand this market is to look at examples. The majority of the pictures in this book are aimed at the promotional market in one way or another, and the two case studies shown in the panels may show the kind of thought that goes into such pictures.

Case Study 1

This picture is distinguished by its attention to detail. The mosque and market made an obvious subject, but it took the low, slanting evening light – always the most moody and romantic time of day – to tie the different elements in the picture together. The haze, the colour of the light, and the mixture of dying daylight and flaring lamps give it a feeling that would not have been possible at any other time of day. The slightly elevated position prevents foreground figures from dominating the scene and obscuring the action, and the mood was accentuated with the use of an effects filter; these can be very effective when they genuinely complement the scene, but beware of using them merely because they make the picture different, which is not synonymous with better. Always check to see if the effect you want really is enhanced by the filter, and if in doubt (and if you have time) shoot several variations, with and without filtration. Often these variations will appeal to the different tastes of different clients.

Case Study 2

This picture could be used on the front cover of a yachting magazine or book, in a travel brochure or magazine featuring exotic holidays, to illustrate an article about romance, to demonstrate photographic technique, or on a leaflet advertising wine. It was carefully thought out and constructed – the couple and the yacht did not come together through a happy accident – and it was planned and executed purely as a stock picture, along with several others which were taken on the same day and at nearby locations. Although this sort of photography is obviously more expensive than just shooting found subjects, and requires more planning, this picture has sold frequently, repaying the initial investment many times over.

Editorial

It is important to distinguish between picture *agencies* and picture *libraries* when considering editorial pictures. There can be considerable overlap, but the distinction is that the agency either originates the story or is commissioned to cover it, while the library merely supplies pictures for someone else's story. Names such as Magnum, Sygma, and Black Star are well known for their coverage of trouble-torn parts of the world, and for a particular kind of photographer: brave, resourceful and willing to share the hardships of his subjects, including being shot at.

Some picture libraries function from time to time as agencies, and almost all agencies maintain libraries, but covering a story in depth, agency style, requires more time and money than can normally be invested in stock pictures. There is, however, a sort of half-way house, where editorial and other stock photography can be profitably combined.

Typically, a photographer will have an idea – such as photographing ethnic communities in New York City. Such an idea really needs to be backed up with words, and unless the photographer is himself a writer, he might do well to team up with one for the project.

In itself the ethnic community project is not likely to produce many immediately saleable stock shots, but if the photographer makes the rounds of editors before he goes, he may be able to gather commissions, or if not commissions at least interest. From the editors' comments and from his library he can get a good idea of what pictures will sell and he can combine his original trip with stock shooting, which will at least offset his expenses and may well pay for the whole trip. Approaching the same problem from the other direction, it may be possible to spend a few extra days somewhere that he is going anyway on a commissioned shoot, and take the editorial pictures that way. We shall return to the

These children, rehearsing for a mass gymnastics display at a Tibetan Children's Village, Dharamsala, not only provide an eye-catching pattern: no two are in *exactly* the same position, which makes it a very amusing picture to study. Although the main use for this sort of picture might seem to be editorial, it is not hard to imagine other uses – and it would make a magnificently frustrating jigsaw.

A very attractive picture from a series on the lesser-known peoples of south-east Asia. It repays close study – not the contrast between the traditional jewellery and the modern wristwatch, or the timeless features of the girl and the baby's Western-influenced clothes – but it is still primarily an editorial or possibly travel shot, though (for example) fabric manufacturers might also find some advertising use for it.

idea of putting such a package together in the chapter on travel photography.

Although some stock photographers may sometimes produce picture stories, the majority of editorial picture sales will be little more than fillers. This is inevitable: in taking pictures of as wide a variety of subjects as possible, it is unlikely that the stock photographer will have either the time or the incentive to try for in-depth pictures. As a result, the best pictures for editorial use are those which show something typical: the pin-striped businessman in the City of London, or the young black man with the huge music centre slung over his shoulder in New York City. There is also a market for the very slightly out-of-the-ordinary, especially if it is reasonably topical or significant, such as the burnoused Arab in Saudi Kensington, or the glue-sniffing punk, and the obviously bizarre or eccentric.

Visual

Chocolate boxes, jigsaws, greeting cards, calendars...this picture could equally well be used for any of these purposes, or for editorial use about travel or retirement, or an advertisement for a savings scheme.

There are two distinct markets for pictures which sell on their visual appeal alone. One is completely predictable and consists of the traditional 'chocolate box' market (pictures for use on chocolate boxes, greetings cards, calendars, or even record covers). The other is equally completely unpredictable, because it depends on the whim or taste of an individual buyer. This second market is seen most clearly in posters, though there is an increasing demand for speciality calendars and greetings cards.

The market for predictable pictures is best served by medium format or even large format studies of safe subjects, rendered with exquisite clarity and technical skill. There is little or no room for experiment, unless you count a starburst filter for a snowy Christmas scene at night as experimental. Despite the apparently clichéd nature of these pictures they are far from easy to take. Some people feel that this sort of photography is soul destroying, or harmful to their artistic vision, because the photographer must learn to subordinate his personal taste and pander to those who like out-and-out clichés, but those who accept it as a demanding test of photographic control and discipline find that they learn a surprising amount about the technical and analytical side of their craft. It can also be one of the most lucrative areas of stock photography, so it is not to be lightly dismissed.

The unpredictable market, on the other hand, can be much more fun. The problem is that you never know whether your pet picture is going to sell, so you have to treat this sort of photography as icing on the cake – fun to do, good for your personal development as a photographer, but ultimately non-commercial unless you are lucky.

As in so many cases, there are areas in which these two markets overlap. For example, there is a school of tacky poster and greeting card design in which Beautiful Thoughts are superimposed on a rather attractive simple seascape or landscape – a bit 'camera club' in concept, but nevertheless more original than a Christmas card snow scene. There is also a modest market for humour, again mostly on low-cost (and often fairly low-brow) posters, so if you have an eye for amusing juxtapositions you can do fairly well here. The same goes for cute shots aimed at a more sophisticated market than the kittens-in-the-knitting-basket audience. Piglets (and indeed full-grown pigs) are a popular subject, and hippopotamuses have their possibilities. For any of these it is important to remember that a poster will be on display for months, or even years, and the picture has to have staying power.

Viewed objectively, this picture is somewhat murky, and the foreground is frankly messy; but it does convey a mood very well. As an experiment, try cropping it in different ways. Does removing the foreground improve it or detract from it? Why? Ultimately, you have to cultivate an ability to rely on your own visual judgement.

This is a double exposure – the big yellow blob is neither sun nor moon, but echoes the golden floodlighting on the Sphinx. As usual with the most successful ''night'' shots, this picture was taken when there was enough light in the sky to read as a deep blue, thereby silhouetting the pyramid.

HARDWARE

The Relevance of Equipment

There is an old saying that it is the photographer that makes the picture, not the camera; but this is only partly true. There are four major counter-arguments.

First, not all cameras can deliver the same image quality. Most reputations, good or bad, are deserved. It is true that some reputations rise and others fall, and that some manufacturers are notorious for dubious quality control (if it's good, it's great, but if it's bad it's a disaster), but at any one time there are only a few names which are indisputably at the top.

Secondly, the camera must be reliable. The same comments apply here as above, but even the best camera can fail, so it is a good idea to carry two or more similar (or identical) bodies

as insurance against this: when you have spent a small fortune chartering a helicopter to shoot New York City from the air, you do not want your cameras to break down! If you intend to specialise in the more rigorous forms of travel photography, it is worth considering mechanical (rather than electronic) cameras, because even spare batteries can go flat and tropical humidity can do nasty things to battery and switch contacts. By the same token, it is worth standardising on the same readily-available batteries for all your equipment, as far as possible, so that you can rob Peter to pay Paul if necessary.

Thirdly, the camera must be versatile. Not only must it be suitable for the work you normally do: it must also be suitable, or adaptable, for

A shot which could be taken equally well on almost any camera, from 35mm to 11 x 14in; the larger formats would pay dividends, though, both in the sharpness of the foreground and in the tonality of the background.

A typical 35mm shot. Although something similar could have been shot on larger format, the spontaneity of the expression would have been lost, and in any case, 35mm is perfectly acceptable for this sort of picture.

The sort of picture ideally suited to medium format. Large format would not be able to deliver the numbers of pictures required – even at a cricket match there is some action – but 35mm could not have provided the quality.

any out-of-the-ordinary work which you are likely to do. An important point here can be the availability of special-purpose lenses and accessories on hire, which is another good reason for using one of the standard professional cameras. Dot not be seduced, however, into imagining that there is any such thing as a universal camera. Many manufacturers claim this, but in the final analysis none of them can deliver: if they could, there would be no hope for their competitors!

Finally, you must be happy with your equipment. This is very much a personal matter: for example, although the Hasselblad is considered the standard rollfilm SLR, neither of the authors now uses the 6 x 6cm 'Blad' because we both prefer the 6 x 7cm format. Most camera stores can also tell sad stories of people who came into some money and bought the camera system of their dreams, only to find that they could not get on with it. There is no substitute for just 'playing with' as wide a range of cameras as possible, and this is one of the reasons for going to a professional camera store instead of a discount merchant. Another is the standard of service – cameras do break down and need servicing, and a professionally oriented store will understand that you need your camera to earn your living. There is a question of expense here, but it is worth considering the possible returns against the outlay: a poor workman may blame his tools, but a good workman will buy the best tools he can afford and look after them.

Large Format

If you watch someone going through a batch of transparencies, nine times out of ten they will separate them into three piles. They will go through the big, impressive, easy-to-see large-format pictures first, then the rollfilm, and only thirdly the 35mm. This alone gives larger format pictures a selling edge.

Secondly, a larger image normally means better technical quality in reproduction – though a lot depends on the film used, the camera lens, the quality of the separations, the final reproduction size, and the photographer's skill. A good Kodachrome is preferable to a mediocre 5 x 4″ any day.

Thirdly, almost all large-format cameras permit the use of camera movements. It is true that a PC or shift lens gives the single most useful movement (the rising/cross front) to the 35mm and rollfilm user, but most PC lenses are very nearly as expensive as a cheap view or technical camera (which is vastly more versatile) and are only available in one or two focal lengths for any given camera, whereas view camera movements are available with any lens.

Large format cameras are not, however, necessarily suitable for stock photography. The biggest single drawback is the running cost. For the price of five rolls of 120 film, processed, you can shoot about ten 5 x 4″ pictures, half a dozen 10 x 8″, or a couple of 14 x 11″ – or three 36-exposure rolls of Kodachrome. This means that the only format normally used for stock photography is 5 x 4″, and then only for landscapes and a few other types of readily saleable pictures, while 7 x 5″ and 10 x 8″ are used only for the occasional sure-fire seller, mostly 'chocolate box' shots. On the other hand, it is common practice to make enlarged duplicates of strongly-selling stock shots, often on 5 x 4″, sometimes on 10 x 8″, and conceivably on 14 x 11″.

The other disadvantages of large format are size and weight, slow operation, complete lack of 'idiot proofing', the number of cut-film holders required; and the comparatively limited range of lenses available. The cost of the actual cameras is surprisingly reasonable for 5 x 4″, though 10 x 8″ cameras and lenses can be a bit alarming, and the mighty Imperial or Deardorff 14 x 11″ cameras can cost as much as a good second-hand car by the time you have added a couple of shutters and lenses.

There are, however, two compromises that are surprisingly little appreciated. One is a 5 x 4″ camera with a rollfilm back, and the other is a Baby Linhof, originally designed to use with 6 x 9cm cut film (which is also still available), but more convenient with a Super Rollex 6 x 7cm or 6 x 9cm rollfilm back. Both offer enough movements to run most lenses out of coverage, and the little Linhofs can also be used hand-held with their coupled rangefinders. Several pictures in this book were shot with Linhofs, a Technica 70 and a Super Technica IV.

Both of these pictures exploit the tonal range and detail of which large format cameras are capable. It is the richness of texture, tone, and detail – the feeling that we can almost reach into the print and touch the subject – that makes 4 x 5in and above so suitable for landscapes of this kind.

Rollfilm

There have been numerous rollfilm sizes in the past, but the only modern survivor is the 62mm wide 120/220 size. The original 120 film is just over 32″ (82cm) long, and paper backed; the newer 220 size is twice as long, but has only a leader and trailer of black paper. Some cameras can accept both, some require separate backs for the two kinds, and some only accept 120. Some cameras also accept 70mm backs, allow-ing 50 or more exposures at one loading, but emulsion choice in both 220 and 70mm is limited and processing is not always readily available.

There are a number of rollfilm/70mm for-mats, known by a variety of names. The most common are known by their nominal image sizes in centimetres (which are not necessarily the actual sizes) as follows:

Nominal (cm)	Nominal (inch)	Actual (mm)	Notes
6 x 4.5	2¼ x 1⅝	56 x 43	Originally 16-on-120, now 15-on to allow a wider handling margin
6 x 6	2¼ x 2¼	56 x 56	12-on-120; popularised by Rolleiflex and Hasselblad. Also in 70mm
6 x 7	2¼ x 2¾	55 x 68 to 56 x 72	10-on-120; the 'ideal format'. Some cameras give 20-on-220. Also in 70mm
6 x 9	2¼ x 3¼	56 x 75 to 56 x 88	The original 8-on-120 format, dating from about 1903

Rollfilm can capture broad sweeps of colour every bit as well as a larger format. It cannot render the buildings as sharply, but this is not pictorially important here – and in any case, the atmospheric haze at sunset would largely have negated the superior sharpness of the larger format.

There are also special wide-angle formats, 6 x 12cm and 6 x 17cm, introduced by Linhof and later copied by others. The cameras using these formats incidentally provide an 'instant rising front', by the simple expedient of discarding the bottom half of the picture. An uncropped 6 x 17cm picture is a memorable sight!

The rectangular 645 format fits most reproduction sizes better than 6 x 6cm, so the quality loss is rarely significant, given lenses of equal quality. Most 645 cameras are aimed at the amateur, however, and some are not as robust as larger models; the 'amateur' image can also influence picture researchers. The quality advantage over 35mm Kodachrome is not particularly great, and the transparencies are rather less impressive than the larger formats, so 645 is comparatively little used for stock photography. Some larger format cameras accept 645 backs.

The 6 x 6cm format was originally designed to allow the use of a waist-level reflex finder (see below). Because few pictures are printed square, pictures usually have to be cropped for reproduction, which reduces the *effective* format to the same as the 645 size. This is theoretically an advantage for stock photography, because the square image can be cropped either vertically or horizontally, but in practice a strongly composed rectangular picture often sells better than a square one in which the picture researcher has to hunt for the composition.

The 6 x 7cm 'ideal format' normally requires a minimum of cropping for reproduction; the effective film area is therefore 50-100 per cent greater than 6 x 6cm. The relatively small increase in size also results in a surprising increase in the impressiveness of the trans-

Unless you are using a square format camera, which allows cropping for either vertical or horizontal format, it is a good idea to shoot both 'portrait' and 'landscape' versions of the same shot, or to take a number of related shots, as here.

parency. This is, therefore, very much the preferred size for rollfilm stock pictures. It has almost completely supplanted the old 6 x 9cm size, which usually has to be cropped to about 6 x 7cm anyway, though rollfilm backs for 5 x 4″ cameras are sometimes found in the 8-on format.

Most serious stock photographers will use 6 x 6cm or 6 x 7cm single-lens reflexes. The actual choice of camera will depend very much on personal taste; for example, some people love the Pentax 67's giant 35mm construction, whilst others loathe it. Three particular points to watch are the availability of interchangeable backs, the type of viewfinder, and flash synchronisation speeds.

Interchangeable backs allow you to shoot on different film stocks, and they can be pre-loaded if you want to take a number of pictures in quick succession; changing a back is much quicker than changing a film. A Polaroid Land back is also a boon for taking test pictures.

Reflexes other than 6 x 6cm will require either a rotating back or a prism if you want to use them for both vertical and horizontal pictures, and either one makes for a bigger and heavier camera; this was the original reason for the 6 x 6cm format. On most cameras, the prism is an expensive, bulky and heavy extra, and may crop significantly into the picture area.

Some rollfilm SLRs use a leaf shutter built into each lens, whilst others have focal plane shutters. Leaf shutters can synchronise with flash at all speeds, but big focal plane shutters may be limited to 1/30 second or slower. If flash synchronisation is important to you, bear this in

mind – though some cameras with focal plane shutters also offer one or two lenses with leaf shutters for just this reason.

Because rollfilm SLRs are so widely marketed, it is easy to ignore the alternatives, some of which make excellent cameras for stock photography. Rollfilm technical cameras have already been mentioned, as have the ultra-wide-angle 6 x 12cm and 6 x 17cm types, but the old-fashioned twin-lens reflex is well worth considering as an excellent means of low-cost entry into medium format photography: a second-hand Rolleiflex, or a new Yashica, may be a little limited next to an SLR system, but image quality is superb and the cameras are immensely strong and reliable.

Another possiblity is the compact, light roll-film folder. The 6 x 7cm Plaubel Makinas, with a choice of fixed 80mm f/2.8 and 50mm f/4.5 Nikkors, are first-class cameras (if somewhat

The 6 x 17cm format is one of the less usual ones on 120, but as this picture shows, it can be immensely effective. Because of the design of the camera (a Linhof), the picture does not exhibit the curiously bulging shape of traditional panoramic cameras: in effect, it is a panoramic 'slice' out of a 5 x 7in image.

expensive), and Fuji's 645 folders are also worth a look. Older folders are not usually a good idea: rigidity is often questionable and uncoated lenses can give a very flat, blue image. Finally, there are the rigid rollfilm cameras such as the Linhof 220, the Mamiya-Press, the Omega Rapid (formerly Koni-Omega), and Fujica's 'giant Leica' G670 and G690, though not all of these are currently in production.

An excellent picture on rollfilm – but on 4 x 5in it would have been even better. Strongly selling pictures like this are often 'duped up' to 4 x 5in, both to increase their impact and to provide additional copies for sale.

35mm Cameras

In 35mm, only the very best is likely to be good enough. The 35mm format is working at the absolute limits of acceptability as far as image quality goes, as can easily be shown.

A full-page magazine picture is about 8 x 11″, which represents an 8X magnification of 35mm. In order to appear critically sharp to a person with average eyesight at an average reading distance (10in/25cm), the resolution in the final image must be at least 8 lp/mm (line pairs/mm). Assuming a perfect transfer from the original transparency, the resolution on the film must be 8 x 8=64 lp/mm; a 30 per cent loss (the least likely in practice) brings this up to about 85 lp/mm. In rigorous tests, using two of the sharpest lenses available, the American magazine *Modern Photography* showed that 100 lp/mm was just attainable on Kodachrome 25; their conclusion was that 90 lp/mm was the most that could be hoped for in normal working conditions with first-class equipment and Kodachrome 25.

Furthermore, a 35mm slide is harder to read than a larger picture, especially where fine

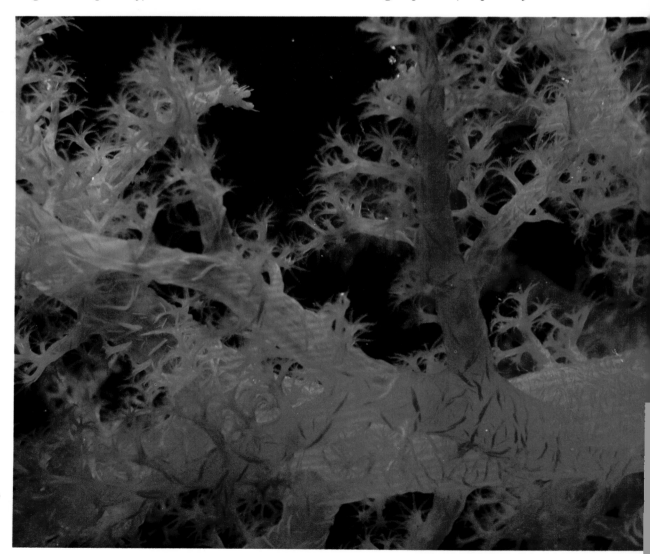

For many specialist applications, such as this underwater shot, 35mm is the only practical choice. Only a very few photographers, specialising exclusively in underwater material, use (or can afford) underwater housings for 120 cameras.

detail, texture, or subtle tonality are involved. Often a 35mm slide can only attract the eye by sheer impact – and what passes for impact in the jewel-like 24 x 36mm frame may not always be what is wanted in an 8 x 11″ enlargement.

Despite all this, there is still a strong case to be made for 35mm. After all, what counts in the final analysis is the picture, and a good Kodachrome is preferable to a mediocre picture on rollfilm or 5 x 4″, unless a really large, technically perfect enlargement is needed. Also, not all pictures need to be bitingly sharp; the graininess

of 35mm can be used to convey mood or immediacy. The cameras themselves are small, light, fast-handling and flexible, and because the image area is small, it is possible to construct specialised high-speed, wide-angle, or long-focus lenses that would be quite impracticable in larger formats. The compact size also allows the use of all kinds of accessories such as high-speed motor drives, and 20 rolls of film – 720 exposures – take up no more room (and are much easier to pack) than a couple of 10 x 8″ cut film holders.

The cost of cameras and film is for the most part amazingly low, because amateurs buy both in huge quantities, permitting enconomies of scale: it would be economically impossible to produce Kodachrome for professionals only. Even the exotic lenses bought only by sports photographers and newspapers ultimately owe their origin to the amateur: manufacturers produce them in order to attract professionals, because a professional image sells more cameras. Finally, the low cost of film means that bracketing and experimenting will not break the bank, allowing more scope for creative and original pictures. It is no surprise that 35mm is so popular, but it always pays to remember its limitations.

The speed with which a 35mm camera can be used makes it ideal for candid pictures, whether of an oriental gentleman using an old German camera or a balloon seller in Agra.

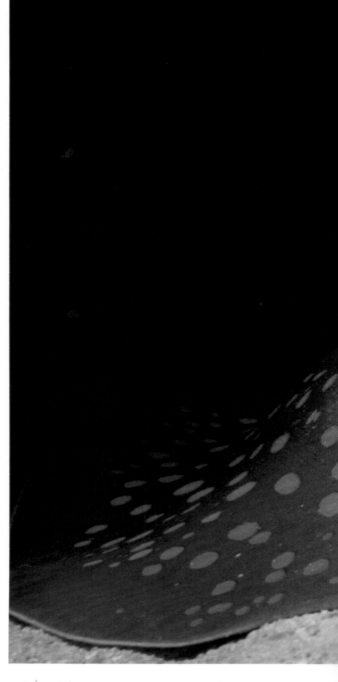

In sport and action photography, 35mm is the norm. Because so much reportage is shot on 35mm, editorial pictures in many magazines (though not often in advertising) are normally reproduced from 35mm, which may therefore be preferred to larger formats. Some libraries handle only 35mm, though they can be at a disadvantage in some fields when a client has requested pictures from a number of libraries. As already mentioned, most will look at the easier-to-read large format and rollfilm pictures first. From the library's point of view, there is however one major advantage: storage is very much simpler.

Upon analysis, there turn out to be two ways of using 35mm. One takes advantage of the fast handling, low film cost, and specialised lenses, to produce the kind of pictures which can best be taken with a 35mm camera. Just compare a Hasselblad ELM plus 500mm Tele-Tessar with a motor-driven Nikon plus 300mm Nikkor. The rollfilm camera weighs a ton, costs a fortune, and limits you to an f/8 lens and one frame per second: the Nikon is (just) hand holdable, reasonably affordable (especially with the f/4.5 lens), and gives you five frames per second. In addition, you can buy a 300mm f/2 for the Nikon, and a nine frame per second motor drive, which you could not get for the Hasselblad at any price. At this point, the unquestionably superior image quality of the larger camera becomes somewhat academic.

The second way of using 35mm is to treat it as a smaller version of a rollfilm camera, with a tripod, Kodachrome 25, and carefully chosen high resolution lenses – never zooms – working at their optimum apertures (usually f/5.6 to f/8). The results can be astonishingly good, though the pictures may sell better if the best ones are duped up to a larger format before being put into the library.

Either way, 'snapshooting' is not going to be enough if you want to sell 35mm pictures: both approach and technique require a perfectionist attitude. If you use *only* 35mm equipment, there are certain fields (especially landscape and 'chocolate box' work generally) where you will be at a disadvantage, but at least you will be able to concentrate on getting the best from your equipment. On the other hand, although larger pictures normally sell better, using only rollfilm or large format equipment may limit your photography unduly. Using both is ideal in some ways, but it means much more weight, extra time spent fiddling with equipment, and the temptation to regard 35mm as the poor relation, suitable only for snapshots.

Finally, if you do decide to concentrate on 35mm, remember that the Leica offers an alternative to the reflex. Although expensive, and not suitable for all types of photography, it is smaller, lighter, quieter, simpler, more reliable, and offers probably the best lenses for that format.

The inherent depth of field of short focus lenses used on small formats makes 35mm invaluable when there is little light about, but the subject is not 'flat-on' to the camera.

An ultra-wide angle to create dramatic perspective effects, or an extreme telephoto to compress perspective and accentuate haze: both are easy with the 35mm camera.

The Outfit

The drawbacks of not having a rising front... This Hasselblad shot is very good, but it might have been even better if it had been shot on a Baby Linhof with a rising front, or with a so-called 'perspective correction' lens. In desperation, Kodachrome 25 and a tripod could be considered with 35mm.

The size and content of your outfit will depend on the type of photography you do, the depth of your purse, and the degree of handiness and portability you require. There are also two questions which you should always ask yourself before adding anything to your outfit: 'How many pictures have I actually missed because I did not have this particular item?' and 'If I owned this piece of equipment, would I carry it with me on a regular enough basis to have it handy when I needed it?' The answers are often extremely revealing. Remember, too, that it may often be better to hire a piece of special kit for a particular job than to buy it; there will be at least one place that will hire professional photographic equipment in most cities, against a deposit of cash, or sometimes equipment to the value of the equipment hired.

The trouble with a very large outfit is not just expense. It is also bulky, heavy to carry, a greater attraction to thieves, and harder to keep an eye on when you are shooting. Of course, if you have an assistant to carry the gear and keep an eye on it, and to change film and lenses, you are not quite so constrained. There is also a good case to be made for keeping as much equipment as you can afford back at the studio, so that you can select exactly what you need for a particular shoot, but the overall aim must be to build an outfit that is as small as possible, while still retaining the necessary versatility and reliability.

The bare basics must include at least two compatible camera bodies, as insurance against breakdown and in order to enable you to use two focal lengths (or two film stocks) at the same time. For rollfilm cameras, extra backs simplify reloading and allow you to use different film stocks interchangeably. The number of lenses you carry will depend on personal preferences (and wealth), but three is the least that will suit most people. Each lens should be equipped with the proper lens hood – even with modern multicoated lenses, the improvement in colour saturation is usually spectacular – and with a protective UV filter if you are likely to work in wet or dusty conditions. The only other near-essential filter is a polariser, for increasing the blue in skies and the saturation of all colours by eliminating most reflections. You should have at least one separate hand-held meter with incident light capability, and a spare as well if your cameras do not have built-in meters. A tripod completes the basic outfit.

A tripod is a nuisance, but it is also invaluable. Used with a cable release, it cuts the risk of camera shake to almost zero, and encourages a careful, considered approach. It means that you can take repeated shots from precisely the same

'Trick' pictures do not always work, but when they do (as here) the effect can be stunning. This sort of 'smeared' image can be obtained in many ways, but this one was actually made without a filter, by tilting the camera about half-way through a one second exposure. A certain amount of bracketing and experiment is necessary, and a whole roll may yield only one usable shot.

place, while varying the exact content of the picture – instructing a model, waiting for people to walk into (or out of) shot, removing a piece of litter in the foreground or rearranging a still life. It allows camera positions which, if hand-held, would be both uncomfortable and prone to camera shake. If you are using camera movements, it is virtually essential. Of course only a good tripod is worth having, and it will be expensive, but it is worth it.

Medium format holds the detail in the stonework and the thatch, even if the lady in the doorway is unlikely to be too pleased with the way her legs look in the picture!

When it comes to expanding the outfit beyond the basics, it is time to return to the questions asked at the beginning of this section. Most people will want at least one or two extra lenses, but if you carry more than five, you will do well to ask yourself how often you use some of them. Some accessories, such as motor drives and special viewfinders, are essential for certain kinds of work and irrelevant for others; deciding which you need should not be difficult. The real problem comes with the vast ruck of other accessories which are available.

The old news photographers' motto was, "1/60 at f/8, and BE THERE!". A picture like this one obviously depends more on arranging to be in the right place at the right time than on the equipment you use; the actual camera in this case was 35mm, secured with a lanyard in case the photographer dropped it.

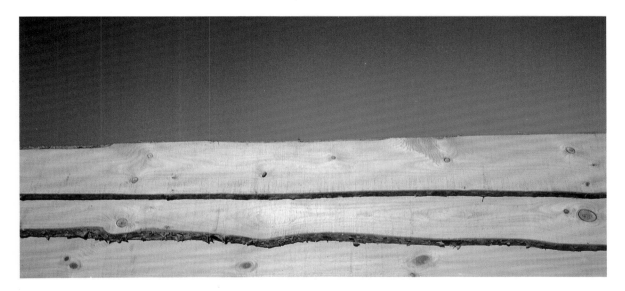

Some are patently worthless, but others which sound gimmicky can be really useful; an accessory-shoe mounted spirit level is excellent for architectural photography, for example. It is well worth checking catalogues and accessory stands from time to time to see what is available, and watching the 'new releases' columns in the photographic press. There is, however, one whole category of accessories which provokes violent debate: effects filters and attachments. Their apologists point out that they can be used to make striking and eye-catching pictures. Their opponents call them banal and gimmicky. Both can be right; it is a matter of the photographer's skill, and the taste of the person looking at the picture. It cannot be denied that these pictures sell, and it is worth remembering that even if you do not wish (or cannot bring yourself) to use trick filters when shooting originals, they may well be worth considering when duping in the workroom.

Whatever your outfit, you will need some way of carrying it. It is fair to say that no outfit case can meet the requirements of both maximum protection and maximum accessibility, so many photographers use hard cases (such as Rox and Zero Halliburton) for travelling, and a soft bag for location use. Both authors use plain canvas Billinghams, which in addition to their excellent design and construction have the advantage of looking somewhat less like camera bags than most other makes, which might as well have STEAL ME printed across them in fluorescent letters. Camera Care Systems and Lowe Pro also make first-rate soft bags; the questions to ask yourself when considering any bag are as follows:

1 Can the bag hold all the gear that I need?
2 Does it offer adequate protection? High-density foam offers better shock protection, while low-density foam provides valuable insulation against screw-loosening vibration.
3 Can I reach *all* the gear that I regularly use, both quickly and easily? Those bags which hold everything in a jigsaw-like interlocking mass are admirably compact, but they are slow to use and can be alarmingly heavy.
4 Can it be quickly and securely closed, yet equally quickly and conveniently opened for use?
5 Would it be comfortable to carry, fully loaded?

You will obviously have to compromise to a certain extent, but only if the answers to all these questions are 'Yes' is it time to start worrying about appearance.

Despite what we said at the beginning of this chapter, it is ultimately the eye for a picture which makes the shot. The picture of the fence against the sky was a graphic composition which caught the photographer's eye by chance, and the illuminated geodesic dome was something which he spotted one day and decided to come back when the light was just right – at dusk, when there was still some light in the sky. But do not disparage technical quality: how would these pictures look if they were soft?

Chapter 5

FILM, PROCESSING AND EXPOSURE

Film

In many ways the film you use is more important than your choice of equipment. The vast majority of all stock pictures are shot on colour transparency film, and unless the library makes duplicates to increase the chance of multiple sales, that film is going to be in front of the client when he comes to select his pictures. He will not usually know or care what make or sort of camera you used: all he will care about is the image on that film.

No colour film can reproduce the actual colours of a scene. The best that it can do is to present them in a way that is pleasing to the eye. Colour rendition varies from film to film, because different manufacturers have different opinions of what looks best. Although this gives the photographer a useful range of choice in the way that he chooses to represent colour, there are many other factors to consider when choosing a film. Among the most important are blockmakers' requirements, the speed and sharpness of the film (which is particularly relevant in 35mm), and the ease of processing.

Blockmakers – the people who make printing blocks from original transparencies – are inclined to be conservative. They know from experience how certain films will behave when separations are made and the picture is photomechanically reproduced, so they set up their equipment accordingly. Unfamiliar films cause extra work, so use standard films where possible. Ektachrome is the standard in 120 and cut film and Kodachrome in 35mm, at least in the UK and North America; in parts of Europe, Agfa films are at least as popular as Kodak for 120 and cut film. There is also a new contender in 35mm – Fuji's 50 ASA material – but at the time of writing it was too early to say whether it really would affect Kodachrome's supremacy.

For sharpness, Kodachrome 25 is still supreme, followed by Fuji's 50 ASA transparency material and then (very closely) by Kodachrome 64. Unfortunately, Kodachrome is no longer available in anything wider than 35mm, so the Fuji film (which is available in 120) is an easy winner in rollfilm. In practice, sharpness is not so important with 120 film because the resolving power of the lens is as often a limiting factor as the resolving power of the film. But with 35mm maximum sharpness is crucial unless you actually *want* a soft, grainy image (which admittedly you might in some cases). As a general rule, the sharpest films are also the slowest. If you need more than 64 ASA in 35mm, or 100 ASA in 120, the normal progression would be to 200 ASA Ektachrome, with a one-stop push to 400 ASA if needed. Many people feel that this delivers better quality than 400 ASA rated normally, though the faster material seems more tolerant of artificial or mixed light sources. For the utmost speed – and grain when it is wanted – there are now several ultra-fast films on the market that can deliver surprisingly good quality at 800-1000 ASA and can be uprated to 2000 ASA or more if required. Incidentally, although ASA speeds are now strictly known as ISO, we have followed usual professional practice and used the old name in this book.

For a grainy and moody picture like this, Kodachrome is obviously unsuitable; a fast film, possibly with special processing, is essential.

A 35mm grab shot; because a picture like this is unlikely to be used very large, the fact that it is on 35mm is no disadvantage in reproduction.

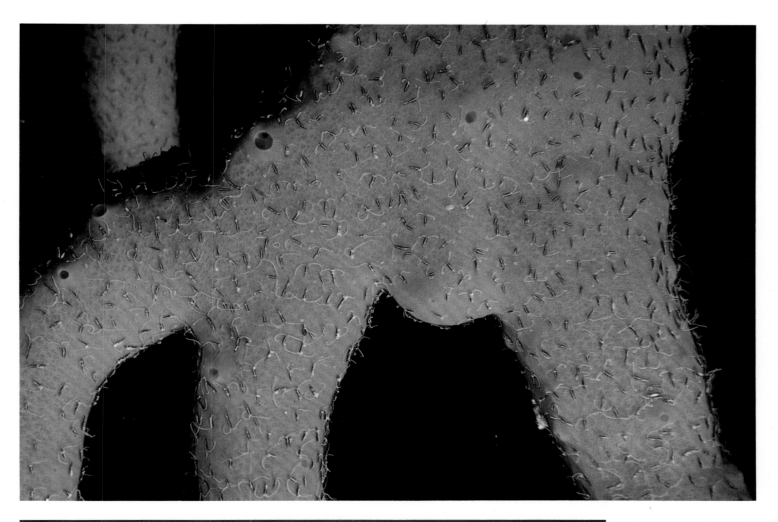

The famous 'Kodacrhome red'. The idosyncrasies of Kodachrome's colour rendition are well known, but modern scanners for colour reproduction can be set up to get better colour from Kodachrome than from any other 35mm film.

Reciprocity failure and colour shifts are always something to consider with night shots, which is a good reason for staying with one film and learning how it behaves under different conditions.

The two big pictures on this spread are both reproduced from 5 x 4in film – and it shows. With the big cut-film formats, choice of film stock is much less critical than with the smaller sizes, and photographers are more free to use exactly the film they want in order to get the effect that they want.

Finally, most professional transparency films use Kodak E-series processing (E-6 at the time of writing), which is available almost everywhere and takes under two hours, dry to dry. Some Agfa films have their own processing, although even Agfa is beginning to bow towards Rochester. However, the real maverick is Kodachrome. This requires an incredibly complicated processing sequence because the dye couplers are added to the three emulsion layers during processing, instead of being already in there waiting to be developed; the method of construction which this makes possible is the main reason for Kodachrome's sharpness. If you live near a Kodachrome lab (and there is usually only one in each country, though there are several in the United States), you may be able to get same-day or next-day processing. Otherwise, it is usually two to four days for the professional film and anything from three days to three weeks for ordinary Kodachrome, depending on whether it is the holiday season or not.

Of the other factors that influence the choice of film, mention should be made of the following: grain size, grain pattern (some are tight, and others are woolly), 'pushability' (because some films respond much better to speed adjustment than others), contrast, tolerance of poor storage (Kodachrome is very good, because it is effectively a black and white film until it is processed), and the type of light for which the film is balanced. 'Pushability' will be discussed more fully in the section on processing (page 63), and it is worth noting that KPA (tungsten balanced 40 ASA Kodachrome) is only available in North America and there not easily. Otherwise, use Kodachrome 64 and a blue filter, or Ektachrome 160.

Several manufacturers offer two ranges of film – regular and professional. The main reasons for this are that manufacturing variations can mean that the actual sensitivity often varies by as much as one-third stop from the nominal speed rating – so a 64 ASA film can range from 50 ASA to 80 ASA – and that films change in colour balance as they mature. Professional films are batch-tested for speed, with the actual speed given on the instruction leaflet, and they are also carefully matured to a fairly consistent colour balance, then chilled so that ageing effectively stops. Professional Kodachrome is slightly different in that it consists of 'blueprinted' regular film. Selected batches are taken from the production line and are much more consistent in both speed and colour balance than the common or garden variety. Any dealer that sells 'professional' films other than

from a refrigerated store should be regarded with the utmost suspicion; you may actually get *worse* results than from the regular non-professional variety. The same is true if you do not store the film carefully yourself. Professional films should be processed within a few hours of exposure, and if they are not, they should be put in a moisture-proof packing and returned to the icebox. Obviously, few travel photographers are likely to benefit from professional films, except for Kodachrome, which is always better than the ordinary variety and comes back in card mounts. Unlike the plastic variety these can be written on easily and do not mark the transparency.

Testing and Processing

This 5 x 4in shot shows that the whole can be greater than the sum of the parts. The cityscape alone is not particularly exciting (though it was shot as the lights were coming on, which always helps), and the sky needed some foreground. Even then, if the picture had been shot on 35mm, it would have lacked the combination of haze and detail which makes this picture so evocative.

In practice, colour and speed variations in processing are usually far greater than manufacturing variations in filmstock, so it pays to compare different labs by sending them identically exposed film from the same batch. They will not match, but even on a simple test some will look much better than others. Choose the one that looks best to you and, if their results are consistent, stay with them. If they are not consistent, either repeat the test or go to your next choice from the original test. It is worth repeating the test at intervals anyway and comparing the results you are getting with the work of other photographers in the library. Once you are satisfied with a lab you can use them to batch-test your films.

Any professionally-oriented camera store should be able to sell you a large batch of film with the same emulsion number (which will therefore have the same characteristics). Even professional films should be batch-tested, and if you decide to use ordinary film, batch testing is all but essential to determine effective emulsion speed and filtration (except perhaps for travel

and some other forms of outdoor photography where minor variations in speed may well be covered by bracketing, and minor variations in colour balance are unlikely to be noticeable because of the lack of any standard tone for comparison). Current Kodak recommendations are that colour film should be stored in a refrigerator, not a freezer, because extremely low temperatures can cause condensation and sticking even inside the original sealed package.

Batch testing is particularly important if you are using duplicating film, photomicrography film, or any other unusual emulsions. Careful tests will also be necessary if you use 'funny' films or non-standard processing techniques in order to get increased contrast, grain, etc. For increased contrast, try the East German Orwo film, or you can push-process ordinary films (especially the slower ones), or duplicate a normal-contrast transparency using non-duplicating stock (duplicating film is less contrasty than regular 'in camera' film). Repeated duplicating will build contrast at each step. For increased grain use fast films, push-process, or process fast reversal film as a negative and then enlarge on to 6 x 9cm or 4 x 5″ print film for the final positive image.

In addition to offering fast, reliable, scratch-free processing (none of which can be taken for granted in an amateur-oriented lab) a good professional processing laboratory should offer speed adjustments and clip tests as a matter of course. 'Pushing' (and for that matter 'pulling') film speed by varying the time in the first developer affects effective speed, grain, contrast, colour rendition and maximum density. Normally a ⅓ stop push or pull will have very little effect except on speed, but even ½ stop is likely to produce a detectable change in contrast. Some photographers habitually 'push ⅓' to clean up highlights and compensate for this with less exposure. Most labs agree that one stop is the limit if you want anything like normal quality and, even then, the grain structure will be noticeably different.

Anything more than one stop may well affect colour rendition and maximum density as well. Results may be just tolerable at a two stop push, but unless you actually want thin and sickly colours, a maximum black that is really dark green and grain like golfballs, do not try

Although you need to know how a given filmstock responds to underwater lighting and filtration, there is little point in batch testing: colours are unfamiliar anyway, and a bluish cast is expected.

For an absolutely 'straight' shot like this, there should be no need for adjusted processing – except perhaps a 1/3 stop push to clean up the whites.

three stops. The maximum 'pull' normally used is one stop, which will produce noticeably flatter contrast. Unless you live in the United States, you will be unable to get Kodachrome pushed or pulled; there, some independent labs offer normal push/pull services, and even the Great Yellow Father will give a 1⅓ stop push at some of its labs. This is designed to save Kodachrome 25 which has been accidentally exposed at 64 ASA (which accounts for the odd 1⅓ stop value, and the lack of other options), but it gives a useful 160 ASA with Kodachrome 64, and 100 ASA with the 40 ASA tungsten-balanced material.

Clip tests are useful when you have exposed a good deal of film under substantially similar lighting conditions; they are widely used by sports and action photographers, and sometimes in the studio. The first frame or two of a 120 film, or the first three or four frames of a 35mm film, are clipped off and processed and the results are used to assess the necessary speed adjustment (if any). The clip test frames should be specially shot, or you may find that the best

picture of the entire shoot has been chopped in half! The lab should, of course, clip the beginning frames of both 120 and 35mm, but it is worth remembering that 120 is not rewound; labs have been known to clip the end of the film, which can be a disaster. If many rolls have been shot, a whole roll may be used as a clip test.

Although most photographers prefer to process their own black and white, it is only very rarely that it is worth doing your own E-6 processing (unless you have a large enough studio and use so much film that you can run your own full-time lab), because a good lab is usually quicker, cheaper, faster, more reliable, and a good deal easier. The time and temperature controls for the E-6 process are very critical indeed and a professional lab's quality control is likely to be a good deal better than most people can manage. The only occasion when it is normally worth considering processing your own film on a batch basis is if you live a long way from a lab and need the pictures quickly. You cannot of course process Kodachrome yourself.

Below
Although this is a grab shot, there is penty of time for bracketing.

Above right
Lighting in places like this is always very deceptive, and careful metering is essential; you may also have to open or close doors, windows, and shutters to get the right balance of light.

Left
A classic Kodachrome shot: a dramatic and colourful detail.

Metering

Even the latest generation of super-sophisticated built-in meters are designed primarily for amateur snapshot use and may not give the best exposure with atypical subjects. A separate hand-held meter, especially when used to measure incident light, virtually guarantees total control of exposure. The old favourites are the Weston Master and the Lunasix/Lunapro, though some new high-tech meters, such as the Minolta and Calculight, are also very accurate. Furthermore, it is easier to get consistent results with a hand-held meter because you rarely know the weighting pattern of a through-lens meter. With an incident light meter, all you have to do is to give ½ stop to 1 stop less for light subjects if you want detail in the highlights, and ½ stop to 1

For difficult exposures like these, you need to meter selective areas and work out which parts of the picture you are prepared to lose as blocked-up shadows or burnt-in highlights. Most in-camera meters would give very disappointing results if you relied on their 'average' readings.

stop more for dark subjects if you want detail in the shadows. If your results are consistently light or dark (and they will be consistent if you use this metering technique), you can compensate by resetting the ASA or compensation dial. A Polaroid back is, of course, an excellent way of testing exposure (also composition, lighting, and whether the camera and flash synch. are working), though it should be used as an adjunct to a meter, not as a substitute for it. The authors both have experience of assistants who would not take a picture until they were knee-deep in Polaroids.

Even after determining exposure with a good meter (and personal experience) it is still a good idea to bracket your exposures – for two reasons. Firstly, it ensures that at least one exposure will be exactly the one you want, and secondly, different exposures have a different 'feel' or mood to them. Often an exposure that is not technically correct will convey the mood of the subject better. Film may be expensive, but it is not so expensive that it is worth missing a good shot just to save a few pennies.

The extent of the bracket will vary according to the photographer and the subject. In the studio, with carefully controlled lighting, half a stop either way may be sufficient. Out of doors, in daylight, it may be better to use a one stop bracket and at night you will usually need to bracket two full stops either side in order to see any significant difference. Usually an exposure ⅓ to ½ stop either side of optimum will still be suitable for library use (and reduces the need to make dupes). With really difficult subjects, such as sunsets, it is worth making five exposures (as metered, and $-2, -1, +1, +2$ stops). Some photographers actually make exposures for such shots at half stop intervals, from 2½ stops over to 2½ stops under. However, with experience, the necessity for this is not so urgent.

Finally, if your meter fails, apply the f/16 rule – it is extraordinarily accurate. Because of the way in which the ASA (now ISO) speed is determined, if you set the shutter speed at the ASA speed (or as close as possible – ¹⁄₃₀ for 25 ASA for example) and the aperture to f/16, the exposure in bright sunlight will be the same as recommended by an incident light meter, remarkable as it may sound.

Large expanses of white, concentrated in precisely those areas where a through-lens meter is most sensitive, will give a badly underexposed picture unless you open up a stop or two — or use an incident-light meter.

Chapter 6

TRAVEL

Introduction

In travel photography, there is a severe danger of over-shooting, because the novelty of the subjects can easily conceal the fact that the pictures are not in themselves particularly interesting. There is also a risk of relaxing technical and aesthetic standards, either because you are distracted by the novelty or because the holiday spirit makes you less critical. If you keep these warnings in mind, it can greatly improve the proportion of successful pictures, and make the whole trip more profitable.

Depending on the subject, though, it is possible to effect a certain trade-off between subject matter and technical quality. For example, the greetings card and calendar markets have an insatiable appetite for snowy landscapes. They pay well, and in many parts of the world snowy landscapes are not hard to come by. As a result, the competition is fierce, pictures are plentiful, and the photographers who sell the most pictures often use 5 x 4″ cameras to deliver beautifully composed and perfectly exposed pictures. At the other extreme, an expedition to a tribe of head hunters could also produce pictures which found a ready sale to magazines, television companies, and possibly even advertising companies or record-sleeve designers. No-one would expect five-fours here; Kodachromes would be fine.

Most pictures are going to fall somewhere

The photographer chose his position carefully, so that the Himalayas formed a backdrop, and then just waited for a monk to come long – a safe bet, as this is the path around the Dalai Lama's palace.

between these two extremes, but the point is clear enough: if your subject matter is unusual enough, the other requirements may be relaxed somewhat. Only with the most unusual subjects will such shortcomings as poor exposure or excessive extraneous material in shot be forgiven, but in many cases it will be enough to have a clear, sharp, well-exposed record of the subject.

Some libraries specialise in the type of shot that is more suitable for editorial use (industry, agriculture, and so forth), while others prefer images that are not tied too closely to a specific location but illustrate a mood rather than a place, and may be more suitable for the promotional market. Ideally, you should shoot both, in order to give prospective clients a choice, but personal taste or specific requests may dictate otherwise.

There are, however, certain requirements and problems that are common to both types of photography. The important thing to remember, as in any other type of professional photography, is that a great deal depends on careful planning, some of which may seem to have little to do with photography *per se*. What you simply cannot do is to assume that you can fit in the odd shot here and there on a holiday – a mistake which is sometimes made even by professional photographers who normally work in other fields. You may be able to get a few pictures that way, but you will not get anything like the sales that would be possible if you organised your time properly.

The commonplace for one photographer is the exotic for another – though it must be admitted that there are more photographers in New York City than in Blackpool, and more in Blackpool than in the average Kenyan village.

Preparation

The most basic and obvious preparation for travelling is to decide where you want to go and what you want to shoot. This may seem self-evident, but it is not as simple as it sounds.

First, find out everything that you can about a place before you go. Read books (especially picture books), talk to people, and visit the national tourist office. If you explain that blue skies are important, they will usually drop the 'But it is beautiful at any time of year' pitch and give you hard facts; it is by no means unusual for a client to suggest a shoot at a totally unsuitable time of year, so check out the seasons carefully. Remember that there can be considerable variation across a country the size of India or the United States, and make sure that your informa-

The concept of licencing hours may be familiar to the English, but a visiting photographer might not relise that they can be a bane; when the light is right, the pub is closed, and when it opens, the shadows are all in the wrong places. Preliminary research could reveal this problem.

tion applies to the part you are visiting. Bear in mind, too, that there is more to dressing appropriately than just dressing for the climate. In some countries women who are not modestly dressed can expect a difficult time, and men with long hair may have problems in countries with more repressive regimes. In countries where you are expected to take your shoes off on entering a temple (or a private house), shoes that slip on and off easily are more useful than lace-up boots, but the boots may be indispensible if you have to walk much.

Check out visas and other legal requirements, and allow plenty of time for getting them. If you have to leave your passport with an embassy, be sure to get a receipt. Never use the mail if you can help it; always go in person, or send a messenger. Going in person is always best because it means that you can sort out problems on the spot.

Also check out customs regulations on the amount of camera gear that you can take in or out of the country or countries that you plan to visit. Such restrictions as 'one camera and twelve plates' are still on the statute books in some countries, and although these regulations are very rarely enforced, it only takes one petty-minded customs official to land you in trouble. Either try and stay inside the limits or find out what you have to do for professional photography – but remember that some countries do not welcome professional photographers, and others will insist that you get a special business visa instead of travelling on a regular tourist visa, which is usually much easier and often cheaper. Try to get the information in writing if possible: one of the authors once had to use an official Government of India pamphlet to convince an Indian customs official (they can be unbelievably obtuse) of the legal allowances for importation. A neat list of equipment, with serial numbers, can help immensely: customs officials, like anyone else, appreciate having their jobs made easier. Views differ as to whether it is worth playing dumb and not declaring stuff: often it will work, but technically it is smuggling and the penalties can be severe, including confiscation or even imprisonment. You should familiarise yourself with the use of 'carnets' which can be a nuisance to organise, but will make your journey through customs consider-

The photograph of New York was taken from the World Trade Center. Tripods are theoretically banned, but a Leitz table-top tripod provoked no objections.

ably smoother and easier.

Whatever you do, insure yourself properly. Travel insurance is surprisingly reasonable, and it covers everything except major losses of cameras, which can be insured separately on a world-wide basis, which is expensive but well worth it. Both authors have suffered heavy losses of equipment, and insurance makes the blow easier to stand. Those who travel only rarely (less than three weeks a year) can usually get much cheaper insurance as an extension of their normal studio or household policies.

What insurance cannot do is to replace the equipment when you need it, so it pays to take great care of it. Ideally, you should carry it with you at all times, but this is not always feasible. In most countries, hotels are legally liable for any valuables which are deposited with them for safe keeping, though their liability for losses from the room may be negligible or non-enforceable, or both. They are sometimes unwilling to take camera bags, but they can usually be prevailed upon to do so. In some countries, theft is so endemic that it is as well to keep the gear as close to your body as possible; a photographer's vest is ideal, especially if the pockets are sealed with Velcro, as the ripping sound which this makes when they are opened alerts you to pickpockets.

Film, specially exposed film, is in many ways more valuable than equipment. Cameras are insured and can be replaced; images on the film will (you hope) go on earning money for years to come, but film can normally only be insured for its replacement value. Film is fortunately much less attractive to thieves than cameras, especially if they can see that it is exposed, so if you keep it in your room, put it in a clear plastic bag: if thieves can see what is in the bag, they will be less inclined to steal it on the off-chance that it is valuable. Alernatively, hand it in to the management. If you can, arrange to have the film refrigerated; a supply of self-sealing plastic bags is ideal for this. Take great care to exclude as much air as possible, especially in humid conditions.

If the worst does happen, and your gear is stolen, go straight to the police and give them a full list of the stolen items in your statement. You are unlikely ever to get it back, but it will make your insurance claim much easier: most in-

In Islamic countries, where people may object to being photographed, a long-focus lens can avoid a great deal of trouble. It can also provide its own unique perspectives, and a means of isolating typical vignettes, as here.

Where people are less camera-shy, and especially during festivities when cameras are much in evidence anyway, a 35mm camera with 50mm or (preferably) 35mm lens allows the photographer to get in among the action.

Leaf-shutter cameras do not always react kindly to cold conditions, and batteries can fail at low temperatures; your equipment needs to be kept in peak condition.

surance companies will not pay without a police report. If the equipment has been entered in your passport, or in a *carnet*, the police report will also make it easier for you to leave the country without being charged duty: one of the authors once had to spend two hours arguing with an Indian customs official in order to avoid being charged 155 per cent duty, and that was with a police report. To be on the safe side, have copies made of the report: difficult customs officials may decide to keep the copy you show them, which could ruin your insurance claim if it is the only one.

Find out if there is anything that is particularly hard to get in the country you are visiting. This not only saves trouble when you arrive, but can help you to choose appropriate gifts to take with you. Women should be particularly aware of sanitary supplies.

Get any inoculations that you need, and put together an approriate medical kit. What you take will depend on your needs, your medical knowledge, and your paranoia; at the least, take sticking plasters, some sort of antiseptic ointment, and anti-diarrhoea pills (*Inodium* are

superb). These can live in the same bag as the toothbrushes, toothpaste, shampoo, soap, dental floss, and sun lotion, but beware of pills in unmarked bottles, which are not only dangerous but can cause problems at Customs. Ideally, carry a letter from your doctor if you require any regular medication, and make sure you have an adequate supply. Carry a few extra to allow for losses and delays.

Budgeting is a personal matter, but it must be approached realistically. Always estimate on the high side, and then add a handsome sum for contingencies; 25 per cent at least, and preferably 50 per cent. Getting more money from home is difficult and time consuming. In many countries, plastic money is invaluable. Visa is probably the most useful card in the world, followed by American Express, Diners Club, and Mastercard/Access, but always try to check in advance about the country you are visiting: for example, few Swiss filling stations will accept any credit cards, though (surprisingly) most Indian hotels will. A major credit card is almost indispensable for hiring cars in many countries, as it saves you having to leave a deposit and may

This picture was 'duped up' from 35mm on to rollfilm — without, unfortunately, making it any sharper.

Technically, this picture is only adequate — but the subject is sufficiently appealing that this does not matter, at least for reproduction at a relatively modest scale.

even allow you a discount. Never leave the credit card itself.

Buying airline tickets is not as easy as it seems. You can save a lot of money by going to a knowledgeable travel agent, but you can also run into a great deal of pain and suffering if you try to skimp matters too much. Some airlines are avoided by all reputable agents, and for obvious reasons these tend to be the cheapest, so always ask the reason when one or two fares are very much lower than the others. A good travel agent is worth more than rubies; if you spend a fair amount on travel each year, he will give you better-than-average service, but you still have to allow for the occasional disaster. Book as far ahead as possible, as this will give you the widest choice of fares, but beware of cancellation charges. If you can afford the time and the money, look out for stop-overs; for a small additional investment, you may be able to get an extra location and many more pictures. Remember too that although 'bucket shop' fares are very attractive, the tickets are usually non-exchangeable, so you are tied to one carrier and possibly to a single flight, whereas with a regular-price ticket you have far more flexibility. The same is even more true of charter flights.

In most cases, booking accommodation in advance is not necessary, but if you are going somewhere popular in the peak season you may have no option. A good technique is to book the first night or two before you leave, and then look around when you arrive, or alternatively to book for a week or two weeks and then cancel if you find something better. There are usually no cancellation charges if you give 24 hours notice, so you are only committed to two days' stay. Unless you are very hardy indeed, or the trip is a very short one, leave the first day free to recover; you will work much more effectively afterwards if you do.

The Travel Package

It used to be possible, in the not-so-distant past, for the travel photographer to arrange all sorts of 'freebies'. Airlines would do tickets-for-pictures deals, hotels would swap rooms for pictures, and sometimes even the national tourist office of the country would chip in. Now, with many more people travelling, such deals have almost vanished. There are still a few hotels and travel companies who will do this sort of thing, but if they do, they will normally make life difficult or impossible by doing it at the beginning or end of the season (when the weather is less predictable and there are fewer holidaymakers around), by putting you in the worst room in the worst hotel in the group, and by demanding so much work from you in return that you cannot even meet their schedule, let alone fit in your own photography.

A few well-established and well-known photographers may be able to arrange a better deal, if they can guarantee publication in a mass-audience magazine, but as a rule it is preferable to arrange the whole thing yourself, if you can possibly afford to do so. This ensures that you will be where you want, when you want, that you will not have any commitments which take priority over your own, and that all the pictures you shoot will be your property. Admittedly, the expense can be alarming, but by careful planning, you can at least reduce the risk to a minimum.

First, make a preliminary approach to the picture library, to get a list of pictures that they need. If you have already been selling strongly, they may make an advance against sales, or even an outright contribution to the cost of the trip, but be wary if they want the copyright of any of the pictures you shoot. Secondly, talk to all the picture editors and other potential clients that you know. You may be able

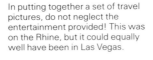

In putting together a set of travel pictures, do not neglect the entertainment provided! This was on the Rhine, but it could equally well have been in Las Vegas.

to pick up actual commissions, but at the very least you should be able to get plenty of ideas about what is needed.

Once you have the ideas, make out a realistic itinerary and shooting schedule. Note the word 'realistic'; allow plenty of time to take pictures, because you cannot be in two places at once (unless there are two photographers on the trip), and in any case it may take two or three visits to get the picture that you want. Never assume that everything will be perfect the first time, and remember Sodd's Law: 'Anything which can go wrong, will; and anything which can't, is only waiting for an opportunity.'

Finally, make the rounds again, this time with your itinerary and shooting schedule. You may be able to jog the minds of the people you have already spoken to (or new people, for that matter), and a well-planned route will at least impress them with your professionalism and efficiency. With any luck, you will be able to shoot enough requested (if not actually commissioned) pictures to pay for the trip almost immediately, and the long-term stock shot sales represent the return on your investment.

It is the details and 'fillers', as much as the establishing shots, which the sponsors of a package want – and which the library can turn to advantage. It is better to overshoot (within reason) than to economise unncessarily on film; the time to worry is when you have too many pictures of the same subject.

Equipment

For obvious reasons, 35mm is very attractive. You will have to carry your outfit, so it should be neither heavy nor complicated, but if you are not going anywhere particularly unusual, you should consider rollfilm. We once conducted an experiment at Fotobank, by sending out similar (and in some cases identical) pictures in 35mm, rollfilm, and 5 x 4″ format; in almost every case, the larger format pictures were the ones used. Furthermore, the larger sizes look more professional, and can often command a higher fee: 35mm can give the impression of being a casual shot, which the photographer would be pleased to see in print, let alone to be paid for.

If you do choose 35mm, a typical outfit would consist of two bodies (at least one fully mechanical, so that you are not battery-dependent and can at a pinch get the local watch-maker to repair it), and four or five lenses, say 20/21mm, 35mm, 90mm, 200mm, and a *good* 2x converter. Any more than this will mean that you are constantly changing lenses instead of taking pictures. A typical 120 outfit will probably be even more restricted; two bodies (and perhaps a Hasselblad SWC), two or three backs, and three lenses is about all that most people can carry for any distance. Some survive with just two lenses – say 60mm and 150mm for a Hasselblad. If you take any more, the most practical thing is to select the outfit you will need for a day's shooting and leave the rest, safely locked up, in the hotel.

With either outfit, you will need all the accessories you normally use, such as a tripod, lens shades, exposure meters, and you will need spares for all batteries, plus duplicates of anything that you can break or lose, such as flash synchronising cables and darkslides for rollfilm backs. Do not forget lens cleaning materials (have you ever tried asking for lens

If you need long-focus lenses, especially fast ones, there is really no possible choice other than 35mm. On the other hand, a modest telephoto such as a 300mm on a Mamiya 645 can produce a bigger and more immediately eye-catching picture.

cleaning tissues in Portuguese?), and a set of small screwdrivers for tightening up any screws that work loose due to vibration.

In addition to the obviously photographic contents of your gadget bag, there are several less obvious things which may well prove invaluable: string, gaffer tape, copper wire, a grease pencil, and a Swiss Army knife (Wenger and Victorinox make the best). Finally, do not forget film, at least twice as much as you think necessary; only very rarely is it cheaper to buy film abroad.

The only way to remember all this is to make check-lists; a sample is given here. Make several copies; leave one at home, one in your gadget bag, and one with the rest of your luggage. This not only reduces the risk of forgetting things, but can also be used at Customs and for insurance purposes, which is why it is worth including the serial numbers.

Believe it or not, this is a 35mm shot. Only perfectly judged exposure and first-class lenses can deliver quality like this.

A fairly ordinary 6 x 7cm original was considerably improved during duplication by adding an overall blue tone and a giant 'moon' (produced with a coin on a piece of lith film).

Equipment Check List

Hasselblad EL/M body PLUS CHARGER	223 456
Hasselblad 500C/M body	234 567
3x120 backs	TT 1234
	TT 1235
	TT 1236
Polaroid Land back	
Distagon 50mm lens	987 654
Planar 80mm lens	876 543
Sonnar 150mm lens	765 432
Komura 2x teleconverter	6 543 210
UV and Pola filters	
Spare lens caps (front and rear)	
Spare dark slide for rollfilm backs	
Camera straps	
Tripod and ball-and-socket head	
Leitz table-top tripod	
2x cable releases	
1x Weston Master meter and Invercone	HH 123
1x Minolta meter	MM 124
Flash gun(s)	
Spare synch cable(s)	
Batteries	
Battery charger with multi-purpose plug	
Lens cleaning tissues; brush	
Screwdrivers	
Self-sealing plastic bags	
String	
Gaffer tape	
Copper wire, paper clips	
Grease pencil	
Swiss Army Knife	

Notes

1 If you are going somewhere that the electricity supply is not reliable, use two 500C/M bodies instead.

2 The table-top tripod is very useful where tripods are banned.

3 Rechargeable batteries are worth considering for the flashgun; you can even get a solar-powered charger if you are going well off the beaten track.

4 Rather than using lens cleaning fluid, *Prophot* sachet tissues are useful for removing finger-marks. Children always try to touch lenses, and sometimes succeed.

5 The Swiss Army knife is considered an offensive weapon by many airlines, so carry it in your *checked* baggage.

6 Carry photocopies of receipts for any recently acquired or new-looking equipment, to avoid customs problems on return.

''Incorrect'' but dramatic exposures, such as this one, often provide a better impression of a scene than a more formal and apparently more detailed picture. In a country like Egypt (this is Cairo), you may be able to achieve more, and with less effort, by cutting the equipment you carry with you to a single reliable camera (such as a Rollei TLR) and a light meter.

Packing

As a rule, it pays to travel as light as possible: this makes your luggage easier to carry, and easy to keep track of. For the same reason, carry two or three large pieces of luggage rather than five or six smaller ones. Use porters whenever possible as this allows you to devote all your time to watching the luggage rather than carrying it and watching it at the same time – but always hang on to your camera case and film yourself.

This applies all through the trip. Keep your camera case with you as cabin baggage, rather than checking it in, as this both reduces the chance of theft and enables you to avoid X-rays in most places. Most airlines will pay only very limited compensation for checked baggage, based on the weight shown on the baggage check: some people put bricks in the luggage to get it up to the limit. Checked baggage may also be X-rayed, often with high-dose equipment. X-rays in general are a problem: few countries allow a hand inspection as of right, and even those that do so in theory may not do so in practice – one photographer of the authors' acquaintance had a gun pulled on him in Canada, and the same has been known in Switzerland. Usually, though, you can get a hand inspection if you ask for it; and as one pass is unlikely to have any effect on most films, the odd occasion when you cannot is unlikely to prove a problem. With modern X-ray machines and medium-speed film, even two passes should be all right, but with fast films (400 ASA and above), all X-rays can be dangerous.

The best approach, is probably to have the film in a quickly removable clear plastic bag, and to allow the security officials to X-ray the case once you have removed the film. This gives them something to X-ray, keeps them happy, and makes the inspection quicker. It is also a good idea to remove 35mm film canisters from their boxes: to identify them, tape the film box end across the side of the canister. This serves several purposes. Firstly, it saves space. Secondly, it makes searches quicker if the security people decide to open every canister (and it has been known). Thirdly, when you enter a country, it reassures customs that the film is not for resale. Fourthly, it saves a lot of time and litter when it comes to reloading. And fifthly, if you tear off the label when you take out

Be careful with pictures like this; even if the couple do not object at the time, they might do so if they saw the picture in print. Either get a model release, or use professional models – and remember that a model has to be old enough to sign a release before the release has any effect.

This very dramatic and striking picture was the result of fast reflexes and a pre-set camera; a few seconds later, and the picture was gone.

At very low temperatures, it is not only the camera which has to be protected: a good breakfast and a flask of warm soup is useful to prepare the photographer.

the new film and replace it with an exposed one, it helps you to keep track of which films are exposed, and which unexposed.

If you are going to be travelling in really harsh conditions, be even more careful with your packing. For dusty terrain, seal everything in re-sealable plastic bags; for extreme cold, consider having your camera 'winterised' by a professional repairer. You may also wish to consider buying hardened cameras: Leicas work very well in cold weather, and the underwater Nikonos is virtually unstoppable in blizzards, rain and mud, as well as in its normal habitat. Electronic cameras, on the other hand, may die completely in extreme cold or extreme humidity, and exposed leaf shutters are very vulnerable both to dust and to cold.

Shooting

If you have prepared yourself carefully, you ought to be able to get in and out of the country of your choice without too much difficulty. You can now embark on the second part of the job: actually getting the pictures.

Some people recommend walking through the places you intend to photograph, without carrying a camera, in order to get an idea of what you want to photograph, of when would be the best time of day, and of what equipment you will need. The trouble with this approach is that you almost invariably miss some unrepeatable pictures, and you also lose the freshness of vision which can sometimes be so useful. The danger of going straight in, on the other hand, is that you will only take what immediately presents itself, and never get around to going back because you have done that subject already. The best compromise is usually to carry your cameras the first time and shoot what seems appropriate, all the while noting anything which may work better at another time of day – usually dawn or late afternoon. It means going to each place twice, and it may mean a few wasted shots, but you will probably get better pictures this way.

Never try to cover too much. It is always very tempting to try to photograph everything, but you are likely to do much better if you have a list of priorities and allow a realistic time for each. This does not mean that you should only shoot to a prepared shot-list – many of the best pictures from any trip are spontaneous and un-expected – but it does impose some discipline on your shooting. This is where close liaison with the picture library, and a knowledge of their requirements, really pays dividends. Almost everyone tries to shoot too much (and carry too much) at some point early in their career, and the lesson is so salutary that few make the same mistake twice.

In order to get the best pictures, you may have to extend yourself a bit. This frequently means getting up at dawn, which is when life begins in many countries. The middle of the day is seldom as rewarding, though there are occasions when the harsh vertical light is ideal, and in some large cities this may be the only time that you get enough light between the sky-scrapers. Then, as the shadows lengthen, the light again becomes interesting. The light of both dawn and sunset is reddish, but the pictures are very different. The light is coming from opposite directions, the activities of people (and animals, and insects) will be very different, and the even-ing atmosphere is usually much hazier than the clear air of dawn.

Effects filters do not always have to be used at the time of shooting; the superb picture of the Taj Mahal, and the eye-catching image of the skyscrapers on the opposite page, were both very ordinary until the filtration was added at the duping stage. By shooting pictures which you know you are going to dupe later, you can save a great deal of location time.

By contrast with the Taj Mahal and the skyscrapers, the other two pictures on these pages are absolutely 'straight': shooting directly into the late afternoon sun produced these golden images. It is extremely instructive to compare these four photographs.

You may also have to do a fair amount of walking or even scrambling, and in order to get the best viewpoints you may have to climb rocks, pathways, and steps; in the case of buildings, you may have to talk or bribe your way in. You will find, though, that most people are astonishingly cooperative: it is always interesting to meet a traveller, and the professional photographer has a certain mystique of his own, so your path may be smoother than you expect, metaphorically if not literally.

Obviously, there are limits. You do not want to offend people, and there are some places where it is unwise to take pictures. Obvious examples are military establishments, which in some countries especially Communist ones, cover more than you might think; dams, bridges, airports, roads, and even military personnel may all be considered off-limits as subjects for pictures. The national tourist offices are usually quite good about this; they will say blithely that there are no restrictions except the obvious ones, and then go on to list all sorts of things which you would not think were obvious at all.

Lower left and right
For shooting at dawn on the Ganges, the only really practical equipment is 35mm. Changing films in an unstable open boat, with no shade, is altogether too much like hard work if you have to do it every ten or twelve frames, though interchangeable backs and 220 film help.

Different cameras limit the amount that you can scramble around. The logging shot was taken with the rugged Bronica GS1, but the Linhof 6 x 17cm camera used for the panoramic shot requires rather gentle treatment if it is to preserve its superb image quality all the way to the corners.

All the time, you have to remember that you are on a business venture. You must balance (for example) the cost of hiring a helicopter in New York against the possible increased income that the pictures will bring; you must decide whether a side-trip to Pattaya will land you more pictures than staying in Bangkok for an extra couple of days.

If you are combining stock photography with a holiday, you can afford to relax your efforts somewhat; if you do not, it would scarcely be a holiday. The authors freely admit that they would never dream of going on holiday without at least half an eye to stock shots, though they would not go so far as one photographer who said that if he could not take his camera, he would not take a holiday. Even so, you should still aim to take plenty of good pictures, and that will mean devoting some of your time exclusively to photography. If you are travelling with anyone else, it may be as well to make specific arrangements to be off on your own for a day or half a day; trailing round behind a photographer can be very tedious, and the pressure from a companion can lead to careless shooting – just shooting the first picture that presents itself, instead of waiting for the *right* picture. On the other hand, a holiday-cum-stock-trip is a good time to try out new film and techniques, and even equipment, because there is no pressure to get a picture and no risk of making a mess of a costly commissioned shoot.

The Establishing Shot

'Establishing shot' is a term borrowed from the world of cinema, where a director will use a clear landmark when he wants to make it apparent where the film is set: in Paris, the Eiffel Tower, in New York, the Statue of Liberty or the Manhattan skyline, and so forth. Sometimes there are only one or two establishing shots that are sufficiently internationally known to be useful, such as the Parthenon in Athens, but in other places there may be many. London, for example, is Big Ben, Trafalgar Square, uniformed guardsmen, British bobbies, and red buses and black taxis.

It is not difficult to make a list of establishing shots before you go, because by definition they are pictures that everyone has seen and knows about. If the library has no pictures at all of the place you are visiting, they will need plenty of establishing shots.

There are, however, two conflicting aims in such pictures. Firstly, they must show familiar subjects in a way that people will recognise, and secondly, they must show them in an innovative way. After all, there are dozens of pictures of the Taj Mahal available to any picture editor, and you need something that will make your picture stand out. A dramatic sky is one possiblity; another is to have brightly-clothed Rajasthanis in the picture, providing a splash of colour against the predominantly cool hues of the building and its surroundings. You could try something at night, or you could shoot with a 500mm lens from the other side of the Jumna river. You could resort to the old clichés of contrasting the richness of the Taj with the poverty of a begger (using a fairly long lens to compress the perspective, so that the beggar does not completely dominate the picture); you could have a beautiful model in the foreground or you could show the ox-drawn lawnmowers that keep the grass shaven. But you must not go too far from the theme: the Taj must always be clearly and immediately recognisable or it will cease to be an establishing shot.

There may also be unexpected problems. For example, the fountains and waterways that lead up to the Taj are by no means always full, and if they are empty, it is very difficult indeed to get a good picture. You have to know what time of the week to go: Fridays are free, because the Taj is after all a mosque, and the grounds will be crowded to bursting point then. The night of the full moon is another favoured time. Not only is the Taj said to be at its most beautiful then, but it stays open much later and the crowds are tremendous. There are all kinds of other examples: the fountains of the Trocadero in Paris normally only play for the first ten minutes of every hour, for instance. Information like this is hard to come by without reading a lot of guide books, and even then there is not a lot

The only one of these pictures which requires a caption for most people will be the one of Toronto — anyone who knows the city will recognise it instantly. Note however that they are all evening shots — one of the best times of day to produce a memorable image.

By making the statue of Sir Winston Churchill the focal point of this picture, the photographer has cleverly blended the familiar and the almost-familiar in what is almost a kaleidoscope of London sights.

you can do in some cases; if there is no water in the pools at the Taj, there is no way of telling when there will be again. Life is like that.

For any establishing shot, though, there are two golden rules: think and wait. Think about the best way to convey what you want to show, and about the best way to do it. Would some sort of special-effect filter be a good idea? What about a polariser to deepen the sky and saturate the colours? A starburst? A graduated filter? How about a double or multiple exposure? You may decide to take pictures with the specific

intention of making a montage in the darkroom, which is a favourite way of adding a dramatic moon. The moon is shot with a 200 or 500mm lens and added to the moonless exposure (taken with any lens) to give a giant moon effect. It may not be strictly accurate, but it can seem more realistic than a straight shot.

Wait for the best picture. Shoot 'insurance' exposures if you think that things may not improve, but remember that sometimes waiting for a few minutes (or even a few seconds) can transform a picture: a cloud clears from in front

In contrast with the picture opposite, the Statue of Liberty stands self-sufficiently alone, symbol enough without any additional material – which is just as well, because it is extremely difficult to get a background!

of the sun, or someone in just the right clothes walks into shot and catches the sun against a dark doorway. When that happens, shoot fast and bracket your exposures if possible; clip tests are the ideal solution to the problem of exposure in action pictures, but in this sort of shot they are rarely practicable.

Some places are very hard to represent with an establishing shot: Los Angeles, for example, has no really well-known landmarks. What you can sometimes do is to find a sign or something similar, that actually spells out the name. The Hollywood sign in the Hollywood hills is an obvious example, but you can also make use of direction signs or street names, or find a building or a vehicle with a name on it – Hollywood High School or the Los Angeles Police Department. Perhaps the California Highway Patrol motorcycle cops are well enough known to act as an establishing shot, but you can never find one when you want one – at least not against the right background. A wide-angle lens, such as a 24mm or wider, or even fish-eye, can be useful for this sort of picture, as it allows you to show some background while making your identifying symbol loom large in the foreground. At this point we are beginning to move into our next category of travel pictures, the 'general shot' which will be discussed later on.

The markets for establishing shots are spread pretty much across the board: advertising, publishing, calendars (though rarely greetings cards), magazines, posters, record sleeves, television and travel. Generally, publishers and advertising agencies require comparatively straight shots, while record sleeve designers are likely to be after something more way-out – glaring colours, looming shapes, and so forth. What they are all looking for is something that sums up one aspect of the place, although the aspect will depend on the market. A travel brochure will want to stress the positive aspects – sun, cleanliness, affluence, and so on – while a magazine might also want to show the less attractive side: jostling crowds, jammed subways, freeways carpeted with an unmoving mass of cars. Calendars might be indifferent to either: thick smog may not be nice to live with, but it can make for some very dramatic shots, especially at sunset, and this might be just what appealed to a particular calendar publisher.

The General Shot

These are the pictures that back up the establishing shots. They show things that are less immediately recognisable or dramatic, but which still say 'Los Angeles' or 'Paris', or even 'Brussels' to someone who knows the place, and give some idea of the ambiance to someone who does not. There are also some shots that are widely but not universally recognised, or require other pictures or a little text to make them absolutely clear: a couple hand in hand on the banks of the Seine, or an old fisherman further along the bank. These are the images which stick in your mind and create the mood of a place. Some will come up in your initial research, and others will only strike you when you see the place, or get to know it; for example,

a coin-operated newspaper machine is not worth a second look to most Americans, but to an Englishman it is something unusual.

Architecture is a typical subject for this sort of shot. You might concentrate on the art deco which characterises both Paris and Glasgow – and who could forget an old-fashioned Metro sign, or a cast iron *pissoir publique*? But you also want people. People at sidewalk cafes are very nearly an establishing shot in Paris, but you find them in Switzerland and Austria too. Go to an English pub and photograph the barman or barmaid pulling a pint (it may be a good idea to ask permission first); photograph the buskers and street theatre that make city life brighter; photograph rural streets on market day. Do not

be afraid to take chances: photograph the giant chess games in the street in Berne, even though the picture may have a limited appeal because the cost of the film is negligible and it is better to have a picture than not to have it – especially if you are the only photographer who can supply it.

The markets for this sort of picture are rather more limited than for establishing shots, but they can still prove very lucrative, and the competition is not so intense, which means rewards for anyone with an eye for the typical. The advertising market is surprisingly wide, especially where the picture is of something typical in its own country, yet out of the ordinary in the advertiser's country. Magazines will often require pictures for editorial use, and travel brochures and articles need pictures to hold blocks of copy apart. There is some demand in television and audio-visuals, as well as in markets such as text books, encyclopaedias, and part works.

Some photographers find it very much easier than others to disguise their true feelings about a place, and this can be turned to advantage by using emotions, rather than trying to fight them. If you really cannot stand New York City, except at a distance, use close-ups to show the dirt, the badly maintained roads, the tastelessness of Times Square, the aggressiveness of the crowds, and even the winos and bums. You may be quite unable, no matter how hard you try, to capture the majesty of Grand Central Station, the sheer energy of the skyline, the relaxed atmosphere of the Village, and the affluence of many of the shops, but you should be able to use long shots to show the good side: the magical sparkle as the lights come on at dusk, shot perhaps from the observation deck of the World Trade Center; the sheer scale of the concrete canyons, shot from a helicopter; the glittering reflections of a sunset, shot from the Staten Island ferry. The only real danger with general shots is overshooting, which is something that you have to live with. There are certain guidelines that you can lay down, such as the juxtaposition of old with new, or rich with poor, but basically you are shooting from the heart. Accept this, and accept too that your ratio of successful pictures to rejects may not be as high as usual.

These two pictures are the kind of thing which you remember after you have left a place, even if you neglect to shoot them while you are there. This is why it is so useful to go to a place several times: the more you learn about it, the more able you are to summon up in your mind's eye the things which make it unique. The 'High Tea' picture is unashamedly posed – but that is just the way the waitress looked at you as she was bringing the tea in the first place.

Inside Shots

Covering a subject in depth returns us to the realm of strict planning. Normally, the aim is the creation of a picture story, which (as already mentioned in Chapter 3) is rather outside the realm of stock photography; the stock shots should merely be a profitable spin-off.

To begin with, the idea must be both feasible and saleable. Feasibility means two things: first, contacting the people who can help you, and asking if they are prepared to grant the access you need, and secondly, being sure that you are up to handling the project. If you have never tried a picture story before, it is certain that it will take longer than you think – quite possibly several times longer. For example, a 'Day in the Life' story will take at least two or three days, and two or three weeks would not be too long to build up a comprehensive picture of a composite single day. If you have any doubts, do not go ahead until they are resolved: blowing one commission early in your career can give you a bad name which can be very difficult to lose.

Saleability is another matter; your library may be able to help, but you will need to provide a lot of input yourself, and unless the story is pre-sold, or unless you are sure that you can also take enough stock shots to pay for the trip, you may be gambling with quite a lot of money.

With these two hurdles over, draw up a preliminary shot list with both specific and general pictures: for example, 'a guard outside the palace' and 'scenes from the market'. Armed with this list, you can go back to your original contact and explain the pictures that you want. Identify any areas of difficulty as early as possible, and try to get promises of specific action from your contact, rather than general assurances. Ask what you have to do, what he is going to do, and what problems he expects. If he does not expect any you should be suspicious.

When you arrive, make friends with your 'minder'; he can be invaluable in soothing ruffled feelings, for general help, and (if there is a language barrier) as a translator. The main thing is not to get nervous; there is always psychological pressure to get the picture and get out of the way, but it is far better to take your time, look for the good pictures, and decide which ones are to be posed (or at least arranged) and which are going to be grab shots. Be as unobtrusive as possible, but if you want someone to do something, ask them politely; most people will be more than willing to cooperate. If you have to wait for a cloud to clear from in front of the sun, or for a shaft of sunlight to strike a particular machine, then wait; if you explain why you are waiting, no-one is likely to object. Always respect safety regulations, and be careful not to endanger anyone inadvertently.

Keep any promises to send pictures (or use Polaroids at the time, though this can get expensive if you are not careful), and write a thank-you letter to your contact afterwards; consider sending a copy to his employer as well. If things go wrong, don't make a fuss: no-one is obliged to help you, and complaining will only make things worse for future visitors.

Covering a 'stately home' such as Blenheim Palace can be done on a number of levels, from a casual day trip to a carefully planned shoot lasting several weeks. The exterior is an obvious shot, and easily obtained; interior shots, especially set-up ones like the picture opposite, are another matter.

Mood Pictures

These are pictures that sell almost entirely on pictorial merit, with little regard for exactly where and when they were taken. Some may be subjects which have been covered thousands of times, such as the snow-covered scenes mentioned at the beginning of this chapter. Others will be pure luck, a happy combination of elements which make an attractive picture. For example, you might photograph a sunset over a bay, which could be used as a background to an advertisement for a 'Get away from it all' holiday, or for a retirement village, or even to sell life assurance. Alternatively it might make a poster, perhaps with one of those rhymes of a supposedly inspirational nature, or it might be used on a calendar, or even sell to a greetings card manufacturer.

Because these pictures depend so much on personal taste, it is hard to make generalizations about what will sell. As usual, a larger format picture is better because it is easier for the client to see when he is going through the pictures, but it may be an enlarged duplicate of a 35mm slide, or even of part of a 35mm picture. Grain, creatively used, can be very effective. It is all very well to talk about luck, but the truth is, the harder you look, the luckier you get – and this applies as much to the 5 x 4″ snowy landscapes as to a scene glimpsed whilst driving along an unknown road, on your way from one place to another. One of the most famous (and most valuable) pictures of all time came about this way: Ansel Adam's *Moonrise, Hernandez, New Mexico*, was spotted as he was driving along, and taken in only a few minutes – almost a snapshot by Ansel Adams standards. Most photographers can think of at least one of their favourite pictures which they came across by chance.

Ask yourself which of these pictures you like, and why – and then try to imagine possible uses and markets for the three. The contrast between what you like and what you may be able to sell can be enlightening.

An attractive picture – but the technical manipulation behind it is masterful, and the photographer is not saying how it was done. There are still some 'trade secrets'!

These pictures can be difficult to caption and file, because the markets will vary widely and it may not matter where they were shot. At Fotobank the computer comes to the rescue, because in addition to the location coding, we also have categories FC (Front Cover), CAL (Calendar) and, as a sub-class to certain subjects, the suffix TYP (Typical). Searching under such headings means that we can find the picture regardless of where it was taken and whether it was landscape (LS) or upright (UR).

Although sales for mood pictures can be very profitable when they do come, they are by no means certain, because they depend so much on the individual taste of the client. Perhaps the best way to view these pictures is as a tribute to your craft and a refreshment of your vision; to be blunt, they prevent you from being a hack. Even this is not always true, because indiscriminate use of so-called 'creative' lens attachments (no lens attachment can be creative, only the photographer can claim that distinction) in an attempt to produce moody pictures can result in the worst hackery of all. In many ways, these attachments make it harder to produce a good picture, rather than easier, because you have to transcend the clichés first. True creativity is a matter of craft as well as of vision, but only when technique comes naturally can creativity reach its full potential.

The techniques used in this duplicate (from 35mm) are a good deal more obvious, but the result is still a picture that is memorable and different from most others of the same subject.

Nearer Home

All that has been said about travel can also be profitably applied closer to home. Few people live in a part of the world so dull, so utterly devoid of visual interest or content that they cannot take useful stock pictures of it. If you live in a large city, there will always be a demand for pictures of it, and you are far better placed to take them than a photographer who is only there for a few days. If you live in the country, you may be able to take pictures which would be impractical or uneconomical for anyone else. In northern California, for example, there are grape fields and wineries, and the citrus orchards. In Cornwall there are the old tin mines, the fishing villages, the clay workings. In Delaware you can photograph fine old colonial buildings, or the Bombay Hook nature reserve, or you can get to Washington in a couple of hours and take photographs there.

With a car, you can easily cover a fifty-mile radius in a day trip, and if you are prepared to stay away for a single night, the radius extends to a hundred and fifty miles. Any more than this, and you are likely to spend more time driving than taking pictures, but at least you can watch local weather forecasts and take advantage of good weather, even at unusual times of year. The Cornish beaches, so crowded in the summer, look their most beautiful under a bright winter sun – even though it would take a masochist to swim in January.

The difficulty lies in knowing what to photograph, especially if you have lived somewhere

for any length of time. One of the authors lived in Bristol for some time, and never really gave a second thought to the local architecture: Brunel's Clifton Suspension Bridge, the Georgian Royal York Crescent, the historic Great Britain steamship, the buildings paid for by the proceeds of the slave trade, the Wills tobacco empire, the British Aerospace works where Concorde was built, the factory that builds the exclusive Bristol Cars, the nearby Severn Bridge, or neighbouring Bath, generally agreed to be one of the finest Georgian cities in the world.

The point is surely clear. A few minutes thought will probably produce half a dozen or a dozen subjects within 10 miles of your home, and fifty or a hundred within 30 miles, at least half of which you have probably never seen. Buy a guide book for your area; you may be amazed to find out about some of the things that you have been missing. Also, the picture library will be able to tell you what is in demand, especially if you can let them have a list of possible subjects: they can make a fair guess at the kind of subjects which will sell, even if they are not familiar with precise locations. The subject list serves a double function, too; if the library receives a request for a particular subject and they know it is in your area, you may be able to go out and photograph it for them. They may commission you or give you the alternative of speculative sales on the normal 50:50 basis. Usually, it is more profitable to take the latter, otherwise why would they bother to ask you to shoot it?

The local paper can also be a useful source of information about what is going on in the area, though if it is as bad as most local papers, it usually only tells you about things after they have happened – not before, when you might have had a chance to go. But if you keep a diary, and enter any annual events in it, along with a note of what determines the date ('last weekend in April', for example) you can build up a useful directory of local events. Dwellers in major cities are usually better served; there is normally some sort of 'What's On' guide, published weekly, or monthly, and the local Chamber of Commerce can be another useful source of information. Perhaps one of the best sources of information is your nearest local tourist information centre.

Agriculture is a subject which the local photographer is uniquely well placed to photograph; unlike the visitor, he can show it throughout the year, from sowing to harvesting, as well as photographing other local industries based on agriculture.

A Bristolian photographer could cover the Clifton Suspension Bridge in a hundred different ways, at different times of the day or night, different seasons of the year, and so forth; such exercises are very useful for personal development as a photographer, as well as providing a range of saleable pictures for different uses. Similarly, different skies can imbue even the very same picture with different moods, different feelings, and different appeal, as below.

The biggest advantage of all is that working near home gives you a chance to practise new skills and exercise old ones, for little more than the price of a tank of petrol and a few rolls of film. You can try a picture story at minimum expense, and if it turns out to take five times as long as you expected, it is better to learn in a place where you can always go back, and which is probably not too critical anyway. This is also the perfect opportunity to experiment with unfamiliar films, equipment, and techniques, without risking an important commercial assignment or spending large sums of your own money, while still working towards a real commercial goal. There are only two real dangers. The first is that because the subjects are so familiar, you may find it difficult to see them with the fresh

eye that is required for most successful photography – though this can actually be turned into an advantage, in that it forces you to make a conscious effort to use your critical faculties, rather than just relying on novelty. The second is that you may have difficulty in taking your subjects seriously – after all, if you have flown a thousand miles to get somewhere, there is bound to be more of a sense of occasion than if you have driven 20 miles, or even walked a couple of blocks. Really good stock pictures of your home town or area can be much easier to take than photographs of faraway places, not least because you usually have a second chance, and the client will pay the same money for them as he would for a similar shot taken by someone who had to fly across the Atlantic to get it.

Chapter 7

PEOPLE IN PICTURES

Pictures With and Without People

Some pictures contain no people, some use people to give scale or context to the composition, even if it is not necessarily a picture about people, and others make people the focus of attention. In this chapter we are concerned mainly with pictures in which people are the subject, but first it is worth looking at pictures that could be taken with or without people, and at the different effects obtained by including them or leaving them out.

We are all very good at spotting people in pictures, possibly as the result of a long-established survival instinct which keeps us scanning our surroundings for friends or foes. We also tend to have a human interest in the people in a picture. As long as the person in a vast and jumbled landscape is more than a cer-

tain size we will always spot him or her, and we have all had the experience of looking at a rather dull picture, only to have it spring to life when we discover the tiny figure that gives it scale and meaning.

If a plain, unadorned landscape, cityscape or room set is the intention of the photographer, he incorporates a figure at his peril, for it completely changes the mood and feeling of the picture. A vast empty desert may symbolize heat, purity and intensity of light, but add a figure and our interest is immediately diverted to what he or she is doing there. As we look at the picture we become less aware of the graphic shapes and the contrast of the yellow sand against the blue sky, and start thinking about the person. On the other hand, a tiny figure in a huge landscape can

Introducing a figure into a shot like this would completely change the mood, and distract us from the light and airy feeling of a forest in the springtime.

This picture was reproduced from a 35mm slide. When using pictures like this, it is essential to scan them very carefully to make sure that they do not contain any unwanted figures, which might be almost undetectably minute on the original.

be a very powerful attention-getter. This has immediate implications for the photographer and the picture researcher. It is obviously far easier to see a tiny figure on a 5 x 4in or even 6 x 7cm transparency than in a 35mm image, so if the photographer wants to try the 'whole lot of nothing' approach, he would be well advised to use as large a format as possible. Similarly, the picture researcher must scan pictures very carefully for people, if this is important for the photograph's intended use.

The appearance of the person or people in the picture, and what they are doing, is also very important. We shall return to this later, but for the moment consider a picture of a sunlit gate between trees. It has different connotations according to who is leaning on it: a pair of young lovers, an elderly couple, a farmer, a group of children. The people may date the picture too – a punk rocker, for example. And are they walking into shot or out of it? Are they looking towards the camera or away from it? Do their clothes merge with the surroundings or contrast with them? The brightly coloured rain-slicker in the subdued landscape has now become a cliché.

Sometimes people are an essential part of the picture, even if they are completely unrecognisable. Imagine a rain-swept courtyard – if it is empty you might not give it a second thought, but with a mother and child running across it, heads bent against the rain, umbrellas up, you suddenly have an interest in the picture. At other times, the picture says different things according to who is in the picture. A photograph of a new office block, constructed of glass and metal, might be a powerful and almost abstract composition with no people in it, but add a child walking unconcernedly alongside it and suddenly you have scale and human interest. Show the same child kicking a ball around with friends and you have made a pictorial statement about the plight of the child in the concrete jungle. Show a secretary eating her lunch on a bench outside and you show what life is like for the people who work in the building; place a girl in a bikini next to it and you contrast the cold, hard, inorganic lines of the building with the warm, soft, eminently organic lines of the girl. Certainly some of these examples are little more than clichés, but they do illustrate how including people changes the mood of a picture.

A clear example of the "whole lot of nothing" school – though the presence of the figure is clearly telegraphed by his contrast with the background. An odd experiment: place the book on the floor (or prop it on a table) and slowly walk away from it. At what point does the figure become indistinct? This happens long before it ceases to draw our attention.

You can find all of these pictures simply by waiting (except perhaps the one of the girl in the bikini). You can wait until there is no-one in the picture, you can wait until a pair of lovers wanders into shot, or you can wait until an old lady is just where you want her in the view-finder. You will often have to wait for people you do *not* want in the picture to get out of shot, or at least to get into the right place, and you will frequently have to wave people on who are politely waiting for you to take the picture before they cross your field of view: often they will not believe that you actually want some figures in shot in order to give some meaning to a rather sterile picture.

There are, however, three major drawbacks to waiting for your pictures. Firstly, you can wait a very long time, during which the light may change, even to the extent that you may lose the picture. Secondly, people may not stand where you want them to, and it is not always easy to give stage directions to total strangers. Thirdly, they may not be the right sort of people: most picture buyers want healthy, conventionally-dressed, happy-looking people, and these are not always easy to find. It is, therefore, a much better idea to arrange your models if possible.

Although the library might want pictures of the same historic monument or beauty spot with a young couple, a young family, children playing and a retired couple, all in similar poses, it is obviously impractical to cart around a minibus full of character actors. Instead, find a young couple and go to the various places of interest that you want to photograph – a couple of changes of sweater or jacket and perhaps a change of hair style for your models will enable you to ring the changes quite satisfactorily. Then, on another day, repeat the exercise with a couple of children, and on a third day, take a retired couple along. Sometimes it is possible to arrange a carefully planned shoot with your library which will include all the variations above in different locations. The shoot may only last a day or two, so you can see the importance of careful planning. The library will want to maximise the number of saleable pictures it can obtain while requiring the whole exercise to be run on a fairly tight budget.

Where do you find your models? You can of course hire professionals, or persuade them that

An occasion when there is not much need for a model release – these Korean peasants are unlikely to see their picture reproduced anywhere! Paradoxically, it is usually the very poor people, like this, who refuse any sort of tip for being photographed.

they need pictures for their portfolio or, for this relatively undemanding form of modelling, you can rely on amateurs. If you do use amateurs, you will have to accept that the shoot may not be as successful or as productive as with professionals, many retired relatives or neighbours would welcome the chance of a day out and you can usually find parents who are willing to let their children go out for a day during the school holidays with someone they know and trust, or have someone else pay the expenses for a day out for the whole family. Young couples are more of a problem, but if you know any students, unemployed young people, or members of amateur theatrical groups, you should be able to secure willing models for little more than the day's expenses and a modest fee each; perhaps no fee will be necessary.

If your subjects are not readily identifiable, or if they are only incidental to the picture (as might be the case on a crowded beach), you should not need model releases. For those who are not familiar with model releases, a sample is given in Appendix 1; this form is basically a contract in which the model permits use of the picture in a certain form, including in some cases the right to treat it as a picture of an imaginary person. Because it is a contract, it must be made 'for valuable consideration', though a set of pictures or a nominal sum (even

a penny) is valuable consideration in the eyes of the law. It must be signed by the model; parents or legal guardians must sign for minors.

The most alarming story about the failure to get a signed model release involves a photograph of a water-skier, which was used in a men's magazine in such a way that it implied that the water-skier endorsed the easy-going and permissive attitudes which the magazine (and its readers and advertisers) liked to imagine it typified. The said water sportsman was, however, recognisable; he was also a member of one of the more puritanical churches. He sued for substantial damages and got them. This was perhaps the high-water mark of such litigation, but it does show the risks that exist. Another cautionary tale concerns a black businessman in the United States who was photographed in the street, and whose picture was then used to illustrate an article about the rising black middle class. He successfully sued for invasion of privacy, although the principle which this case established has since been overturned in the state in which it occurred. As a result of these cases, some magazines now insist on seeing a model release for all pictures in which the people are identifiable, no matter what the pictures are to be used for. On the other hand, it has been held that *paparazzi* using long-focus lenses to photograph celebrities were not guilty of invading privacy, because celebrities should expect this sort of treatment.

In almost every country in the world there are similar anomalies and discrepancies but, as a general rule, it is fair to assume that unless you are trespassing when you take the picture (and sometimes even then), you can photograph anyone doing anything and reproduce it freely, subject to two conditions. The first is that you must not ascribe to your subject opinions or views which he or she does not hold, and secondly, you must not bring them into disrepute in any way. This does not mean that the picture cannot be used for advertising, but it does mean that you have to be very careful what you say. Most libraries insist that a model release should accompany all pictures (you may wish to have the model sign two – one for your records and one for the library's), and that if a model release is not available this should be noted on the caption.

Above
This is almost two pictures in one;
the couple, and the background.
Consider how the background
would look without people, or
with different people in the
foreground; imagine how the
couple would look against a
beach, a suburban street, a wood.

Right
Allendale, looking towards Alston;
without the two figures, there
would be no picture here at all.

The Body Beautiful

Valid feminist protests notwithstanding, there is a tremendous demand for pictures of pretty girls. The men's magazines spring immediately to mind, as do calendars, but they are also used on posters, advertisements, holiday brochures and general-interest magazines.

The first thing to realise is that the market for pictures of girls is not just one market, but many, each with its own demands, preferences, and prejudices. The second is that the competition is so fierce that standards are very high indeed. If you want to see just how easy it is to produce a disastrous and unappealing picture, buy one of the men's magazines that feature readers' pictures of their wives and girlfriends.

The men's magazine market is probably the most specialised and the most revealing. In many of them, explicit detail is the order of the day. Furthermore, because such pictures are normally sold in sets, rather than as single shots, the whole approach to marketing is somewhat different. Accordingly, although much of what is said here applies equally to photography for men's magazines, we have concentrated mostly on the kind of pin-ups that most libraries sell for general use; there is a separate section on picture sets for men's magazines later in this chapter, on pages 116 and 117.

The rest of the market consists mainly of

Below
The lighting is cold and blue, and rather cruel; the model's body looks fine, but her facial structure is not flattered and her neck looks too tense.

Above
There is an air of mystery in the picture above; it looks cold (as the model's nipples confirm), but we cannot help wondering who the model is, and why she is there.

Left
A picture of one girl in this rather strained and old-fashioned pose would not attract a second glance, but this "chorus line" is peculiarly eye-catching, not least because of the repetition of the pattern.

two types of picture: the very modest 'swimsuit' picture, suitable for both editorial and advertising use in a family magazine, and the slightly (or considerably) more revealing sort of picture which can be used to spice up almost anything, from after-shave advertisements to company calendars. Because the model is clearly recognisable, and because such pictures are often used for advertising, a model release is essential.

There are other types of pictures too. For example, the nudist magazines require apparently casual shots of all ages and both sexes, and there are pictures of male pin-ups which are usually designed to appeal more to male homosexuals than to women. Both of these markets are very specialised, with only a few libraries handling suitable pictures, and there are major pitfalls awaiting the unwary; for example, in many countries you are breaking the law if you photograph young children of either sex in the nude. Designed to curb child pornography, these laws can also catch the innocent photographer. The definition of 'child' may surprise you too; in England it is 16, but in some American states it is 18 or even (depending on your reading of the law) 21. Only if you are very interested in photographing nude men or children is it worth pursuing this sort of photography. Often the commercial returns are poor.

This picture is a recreation of something which actually happened during a model shoot; the two girls looking out of the window was such an appealing image that the photographer asked the girls to repeat the pose for the benefit of the camera.

Left
The poses are fine, but the building is not; instead of looking attractively weathered, it just looks like a slightly unsavoury agricultural building. Look at the hinges and sill.

Models

A top female model can earn as much in a day as most girls can earn in a couple of months. It might seem, therefore, that the use of professional models for speculative stock photography is, to say the least, rash. But it is not as simple as this. In practice it is often possible to persuade a model who is working on a commissioned shoot to stay on for a couple of hours (or even a couple of days, on location), in return for cash payment. The agencies do not really like this, because they are losing their cut, but they know that it is widespread, and unless a particular photographer or model really abuses their tolerance they generally ignore it. Alternatively, it may be possible to negotiate a reduced fee – both the models and the agency would rather receive a reduced fee than no fee at all, especially if the model is free for a day or two between other bookings – or to work on the basis of a reduced fee plus a royalty, whereby the girl is given an extra fee each time the picture is used. You may also be able to persuade a model (especially a newcomer) to work for pictures;

she needs pictures for her portfolio, and when anything you shoot is published she will have a 'tear sheet' to add to her book – an obvious advantage when looking for more work.

Professional models are invariably easier to work with than amateurs. They expect to be directed and can usually accept direction. They are rarely afflicted with false modesty or coyness, though they are entitled to draw the line at the poses they will adopt. If you are hiring a professional it is usually as well to make the nature of the picture clear at the outset, although if she is working only for pictures there has to be more give and take. If the photographer is inexperienced at this sort of work the only practical course is to work with a professional model, because he can learn from her. It would, however, be a very rash photographer indeed who went straight into glamour work without serving an apprenticeship as assistant to an established glamour photographer, even if the work was unpaid. As Groucho Marx once said about working backstage at the strip joint: 'The

Inflation? Pictures of two girls together are quite common, and appeal to many men; but three together opens up whole new realms of eroticism. The variation in pose – two supine and one prone – is interesting; how would it look if they were all lying the same way up?

money's not much – ten dollars a week – but it's all I could afford.'

Another difficulty in working with amateurs is actually finding them. After all, how many girls do you know who are as attractive as the ones who regularly appear in the men's magazines, or who fill the pages of the model catalogues? Nevertheless, it is possible to find new talent, and a good photographer/model relationship can be of mutual benefit. A tried and tested approach is to give your card to any girl you think is promising, or even a photocopied or printed letter with your name and telephone number on it, and ask her to ring you at your studio (not at home) if she is interested in modelling.

One final caution deals, once again, with model releases. Many top models will refuse to sign a 'general' model release, but will limit the use of pictures to projects or campaigns specified beforehand – a so-called 'limited release' – so read the small print carefully and negotiate hard if need be.

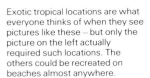

Exotic tropical locations are what everyone thinks of when they see pictures like these – but only the picture on the left actually required such locations. The others could be recreated on beaches almost anywhere.

Preparation

Because pin-up photographs are so apparently familiar, it is easy to forget that they require a great deal of preparation. You need a model, equipment, an understanding of posing and, above all, a clear image of the sort of pictures you want.

The model has already been discussed but, as an aside, it is worth noting that if you are using an amateur model you may do well to stick to comparatively modest shots at first; as the girl's confidence in herself as a proper model grows she will probably become less inhibited. The confidence-building process can be speeded up by shooting plenty of Polaroids – seeing herself in photographs is one of the main things which persuades a girl that she is a real model.

Pin-up pictures are almost invariably shot on rollfilm, because the larger format is much better at representing texture. Texture is often vital in this sort of work, whether you want to convey the softness and hue of the model's skin, the sensuous sheen of satin, or the velvety sand and exotic vegetation of a location shoot in the tropics. On location, in brilliant sunshine, Kodachrome 25 is also worth considering. Quality can rival rollfilm at normal reproduction ratios and because of the jewel-like quality of the 35mm image it is not necessarily at a disadvantage when it comes to selling, but experience has shown that for studio shots rollfilm sells far better.

On location, it is usually best to keep equipment to a minimum, expecially if you have to carry it any distance. Collapsible Lastolite reflectors are very useful, and if you are at a sea-and-sand location, it is worth having a sealed-leg Benbo tripod. Alternatively, use wooden-leg cine tripods. The havoc that salt water can wreak on conventional light-alloy tripods has to be seen to be believed, especially on a warm day and with the aid of a few grains of sand. Any tripod must, of course, be rinsed carefully with fresh water at the end of the shoot. Studio equipment is obviously subjected to rather less strain and need not be as portable; full size 8 x 4ft flats can be used as reflectors, for example. Amateurs working with temporary studios or indoor locations are probably best advised to use available light, perhaps with fill-in flash, if they do not have portable flash gear with modelling lights; attempting multi-flash lighting with small flashguns is difficult and can never equal the results

This is a much more modern picture than the one on the opposite page – but where could you find a room set like that?

obtainable with professional equipment.

Posing is something that the model should understand, but if you are working with an amateur it is worth telling her a few simple principles, such as supporting her weight on the thigh or arm furthest from the camera, pointing her feet in line with her legs to make them look longer, and taking care to avoid poses which make her ribs look too prominent. Amateur models may adopt poses that are almost parodies of the ones they have seen in pin-up pictures: in fact, as many girls have to be restrained from overdoing things as have to be encouraged to pose more provocatively.

Finally, deciding the kind of picture you want will depend on your inclinations, the model's appearance and the market you are aiming for. As a rule, it is best to try for the kind of pictures that you personally find erotic; if you try to emulate the work (say) of Helmut Newton, without having any real sympathy for the style, the result will probably be an empty pastiche.

An excellent picture, if a little in the 'arty' tradition, but it would probably be better still if it had been shot on 120 instead of 35mm. Using clothes and other props to cover the sun in silhouette and semi-silhouette shots is a time-honoured and very effective approach.

Studios and Indoor Locations

The main difference between studio and indoor location shots lies in the complexity of the surroundings. In most studio pictures simplicity is the keynote: surroundings, if any, are suggested rather than constructed in full. At the very simplest there may be nothing more than a roll of seamless background paper, which is the classic set-up for a newspaper-style pin-up, though it does focus attention mercilessly both on the model's charms and on technical quality.

Very simple sets can be constructed, but if you want a full room set, it it usually easier to find one and shoot on location. Some locations can be too cluttered; if you borrow a luxurious bedroom, for example, you may find that you have to remove Kleenex boxes, bedside clocks and the like, whilst in the drawing room there may be magazines and newspapers which have to be weeded out before you can start. And because houses are designed for living in, rather than as

This type of shot can only easily be created in a studio, with a dead black background and carefully controlled lighting; trying to emulate it at home would be very hard work indeed.

By contrast with the picture on the previous page, this is very much a location shot: the water-pump must have weighed a quarter of a ton, as well as being firmly fixed to the floor and wall.

photographic sets, there are perennial problems with electric wall sockets, doors, windows, and other architectural features that are in the wrong place. Some photographers are equally at home in the studio and on location; others have a marked preference for one or the other.

Finding locations can be a problem; few can afford the approach adopted by one well-known Californian photographer whose house was specifically designed, built, and furnished to provide as many photographic opportunities as possible. Location-finding agencies are expensive and variable; if they are to be of any use you must get to know them well and they must get to know your requirements and preferences. Many photographers never bother with them, but rely on friends and friends-of-friends instead.

Whether you choose a studio or indoor location, you must make sure that there is somewhere for the model to dress and undress. Even models accustomed to working in the nude prefer privacy, because they are not hired as striptease artists. Toilet facilities must be provided and, if it is a long shoot, so must food and drink. When on location, check local eating-houses in advance, or take a picnic. When you are shooting in a private house or apartment, even if you are paying for it, it is only common courtesy to clear up and be ready to leave at the agreed time.

The model must of course know what (if anything) she is expected to bring, and amateur first-timers need to be reminded of the marks that too-tight clothing can leave on the body; such marks can take up to three hours to vanish, during which time you may not be able to use the model. The photographer may bring various props too, and unless you are working in your own studio, checklists are invaluable, especially if you are relying on an assistant to pack your gear for you.

Directing the model is a very personal matter and depends on the relationship (which is usually established early on) between model and photographer. Some like to flirt, some like to keep the arrangement formal, and some like a pupil/teacher relationship where the photographer tells the model firmly what to do. Although the photographer should be prepared to lead, he should also be prepared to modify his approach in the light of the model's reactions.

The basketwork screen is the only unusual feature in this picture, but it has been used to excellent effect.

Lower
One of the biggest difficulties in setting up pictures in public places is the public, who are inclined to get in the way, kick the tripod and lights, and get into shot. The proprietors of the restaurant in this shot were much less trouble!

113

Outdoor Locations and Travel

With outdoor locations, there are three main problems: transport, equipment and privacy. If the shoot involves foreign travel, you will also have the usual problems of bureaucracy, passports (find out the name in the model's passport, so that the airline tickets coincide) and *carnets* as described in Chapter 6. There are agencies which will handle the basic preparation, but even the best of these cannot forsee every difficulty.

It is usually best to arrange transport for the model yourself, rather than to expect her to make her own way to the location, in order to avoid misunderstanding and delays. If the location is really out of the way, remember that long walks are tiring and time-consuming, and that the model should not be allowed to carry anything: camera bag handles can mark hands, and

shoulder straps can be ferocious, as an inspection of your own shoulder will confirm! A four-wheel drive vehicle can be invaluable, but always check first that off-road driving is legal, because environmental protection laws prohibit this in many places.

At the location, establish a work bench area, such as the trunk of the car or a sheet spread on the ground. An assistant can keep track of the equipment most of the time, but if there is any danger of wind-blown sand, it is best to work from a large compartmentalised case such as an Adapt-All. The car is also a useful changing room; a white sheet weighted at the corners can be thrown over the roof and windows to provide privacy and to help keep the interior cool. Of course, heat is not always the problem: if you are shooting on a cool or cold day take along some

Cameras and salt water do not mix well, so if you are trying low-angle shots like this it pays to use a waterproof camera housing – or take out insurance.

Pictures such as this one are suprisingly hard to come by, and a library which can deliver them has a marked advantage. An old-fashoned ramble with a group of dedicated hikers can produce many good pictures, if only the photographer is up to it!

soft blankets (or even duvets or sleeping bags), and hot coffee or soup. Drink alcohol sparingly, because it increases the rate of heat loss and can also lead to flushed faces, or worse.

Finally, watch out for spectators and local blue-noses. Spectators can be avoided by choosing a suitably remote location, or working early in the morning, and your assistant can shepherd away any that do get in the way. The models will not usually be too worried, and indeed some have been known to revel in the attention. Bluenoses are more of a problem. Check the law first: in many countries it is perfectly legal for young ladies to stand about in the nude (though not usually young gentlemen), but in others it is not. Even if it is, as in England, there are always such charges as 'causing a disturbance' if the spectators get too carried away. Aside from the law, there is the general level of public morality to be considered; some people will go to extraordinary lengths – using binoculars or taking up a precarious position in a tree – if they cannot be offended any other way.

Signs in the background can be a very useful way of establishing where the picture is set, and establishing a holiday background.

The Picture Set

The picture set, as understood in pin-up terms, is a set of pictures related to a central theme. It bears a faint resemblance to an in-depth picture story, except that the story is insubstantial and almost invariably totally artificial. Sometimes the only real linking factor will be the model, or there may be some theme. Because the theme is normally in the nature of a fantasy, it is very much a matter of personal taste: three different men might react very differently to three different picture sets based on a nude bicyclist, a school-girl and a girl camping.

The photographer who wants to create a picture set walks a difficult tight-rope. Only rarely will the story line be clear cut, as this removes a part of the element of fantasy which many readers will want to inject for themselves; the story should be suggested rather than spelt out. On the other hand, he must not lose sight of

In any picture set, there is usually a progression from the more decorous pictures to the more explicit; exactly where you start, and the route you take, will depend on the market you are aiming at.

his theme, or the set will disintegrate into a collection of unrelated pictures.

The obvious market for these picture sets is, of course, the men's magazines. Each magazine (of which there must be a dozen monthlies in England alone) publishes anything up to half a dozen sets in each issue, so even after you have discounted the comics aimed at amateur gynae-cologists, there is obviously a considerable demand. They usually want a strip sequence, with the girl in varying states of undress in different pictures, and some magazines call for very revealing pictures indeed as the climax of the set.

Although a few models specialise in this sort of peep-show picture, it is rare. The main reasons are the danger of over-exposure (an appropriate term), where the model has appeared so often the publishers do not want to use her again, and the fear that some models have that this sort of thing will harm their serious modelling careers. This is a happy hunting ground for amateur models who are in it for fun and a handful of cash. The photo-graphers, on the other hand, are almost all seasoned professionals, as is shown by the way in which the same by-lines appear again and again in the better magazines. The rewards can be very high, and because the market is comparatively small, many specialists in this field prefer to sell their picture sets themselves – though they may lose out on repeat sales and will almost certainly lose on spin-off sales, calendars and so forth. In a sense, picture sets are the outer edge of stock photography. Although they are speculative they are shot with a single market in mind, and sell only to that market. On the other hand, it is perfectly feasible to shoot stock pictures at the same time as picture sets and to put the pictures into stock after they have been sold as sets.

There are actually two other markets for pin-up picture stories, namely nudist/naturist magazines, and some European general interest magazines, such as a *Neue Illustrierte Revue*, but they generally demand a much stronger story line and a words and pictures package, which puts them in the league of journalism rather than stock photography. Some calendars are also derived from picture sets, and this can also be a very lucrative market.

It is obvious where this shot is leading...the fantasy of the "rich man's plaything" is one of the best-established in picture sets.

Character Models

A less obvious market than the traditional pin-up, although often just as lucrative, is for pictures of people 'as they really are'. Advertisers, audio-visual producers, magazine picture editors and so on require pictures of people going about their daily life – shopping, cooking, taking holidays. They may also want a particular type of person such as a postman, policeman, ballet dancer or artist; the range of potential markets is enormous.

Some categories are very much more saleable than others. Couples in romantic locations always sell well, and family pictures often do even better; a common request is for a picture of a family, walking in the country. What all these pictures have in common is a quality of slightly exaggerated and improved-upon 'every-day-ness'. If you look at the family pictures that you see published, you will find that the couples are usually young, healthy, and middle-class, dressed fairly conventionally (extreme fashions date too fast), with two children – a girl and a boy – about three or four years apart in age, perhaps six and ten years old.

It might seem that this sort of picture is barely distinguishable from reportage, and it is true that for candid or 'grab' shots the techniques are similar, but character photography is not reportage, as it is concerned with the single telling image rather than with reporting a whole situation, which may or may not be typical. The distinction lies as much in the attitude of the photographer as anything else; whereas a single day at a beach or popular resort could produce a number of typical and amusing pictures, a true photojournalistic approach would probably require repeated trips to the same beach, gradually building up a set of related pictures which told a story about its characters and characteristics.

In practice the difference is greater than this. Because of model release problems, it is usual to set up character pictures with a great deal of forethought and care, except perhaps in third world countries where (for example) a picturesque Bedouin or Yoruba would be unlikely to see the published picture, let alone to sue. For some shoots professional character models can be hired; there are actually women who specialise in looking as if they have headaches (for the manufacturers of pain-killers) or men who exude the bonhomie of the innkeeper.

For the latter, it is worth noting that many innkeepers look the part even better than professional character models, and are less expensive. Only rarely will it be worthwhile hiring character models specially for a stock session, but it is often possible for stock photography to ride on the back of a commissioned shoot. If you do use amateur models, so that the shots really are spontaneous, get them to sign a model release; often they are so taken with the idea that a nominal sum is enough. You can buy (or have printed) small pads of model releases, about the size of a pocket notebook.

Couples, and young families, are a tremendous help in selling shots for holiday brochures.

Someone like this painter always adds a bit of 'local colour' and shows that a resort can appeal to the more reflective sort of person as well as to the disco dancer or sunbather.

Everyday Life

The number of scenes which you can shoot from 'everyday life' is endless, but you may have difficulty in finding exactly the picture you want. For example, the often-caricatured 'City gentleman' with his pin-striped trousers, bowler hat, and neatly-rolled umbrella, still exists, but getting a picture of him against the right background (such as coming out of the door of the Bank of England) may require a considerable amount of waiting. The same is true of someone washing a car, mowing a lawn or peeling vegetables, and doubly true of the uniformed nanny walking her pram, or children playing football in a back street. Even if you are sure you know where to look for them, they are impossible to find when

you want them. This is why so many of these pictures are actually easier to set up than to capture spontaneously. It can be expensive to hire models and costumes, but if you plan the shots carefully the speculative element inherent in stock photography can be considerably reduced and the returns can be very good. If the stock shots *are* riding on the back of a commissioned shoot, you have to be careful that they are not too close to any of the commissioned pictures, otherwise the client may justifiably be annoyed to see his ideas being used elsewhere. The question of the limited model release is usually less of a problem with character models than with pin-ups.

An old lady, a British bobby, a Korean mother and child, a selection of bread for sale in France: all absolutely typical images, but often so fleeting or familiar that we never give them a second thought. These are the images which really make up a country – and ones which can be captured by anyone with an eye for the commonplace, and the ability to show it simply and unaffectedly.

It is often more practical to go for a semi-staged shot, going to a place where you know that there is a good chance of finding the kind of person that you want and, when you have found a suitable model, asking them to pose for you. Explain quite openly that you want a picture of someone at the entrance to a subway station, or a roller-skater, or even a man or woman carrying their weekend shopping. Some will refuse, and a few may be downright hostile, but plenty of people will accept. You can judge from their attitude whether or not to ask for a model release, but if they ask for a copy of the picture, jump at the chance. You can ask them to put their address on the back of the model release, and a copy of the picture (duped on to negative stock and printed on a standard package deal) will constitute 'valuable consideration'.

Do not just consider outside scenes; think of interiors too. There is a steady demand for pictures of people at work – secretaries, executives, computer operators, checkout operators, and almost anything else you can think of – although getting this sort of picture will normally involve slightly more work than out-of-doors shots, because you will need to get permission from the employer or local chief executive as well as from your sbject. Just one word of warning: be careful when dealing with young women – you have to admit that a request to take someone's picture does sound very like an attempt at a pick-up.

Domestic and Household

You may be able to talk your way into the office of a complete stranger, but the same approach is hardly practicable with private homes. You may of course decide to use professional models and engage a location finding agency to find the surroundings for you, but an alternative is to make use of a fascinating phenomenon which was discovered a few years ago. This involved handing out letters to people, with the name of the addressee and a few details about them and a rough decription of where they lived, but no exact address. The letters were to be delivered by passing them on to a friend who lived some-where near the recipient, who would in turn pass them on again until they reached the addressee. The extraordinary thing was the speed with which this chain action was completed, and the shortness of the chains. The vast majority of letters were delivered in fewer than ten steps, many in under five.

In other words, the chances are that you know someone who would be a suitable model, and someone else (or even the same person) who can furnish the location. Or you may be able to use the friends' location, but hire professional models. Even if you do not know anyone personally, you have only to ask the person you know who *best* meets your requirements if they would recommend one of their friends. Just think how often you have been able to put someone in touch with someone else who had the information or goods that the first person wanted. One of the authors, for example, was once asked if he knew the whereabouts of a Merlin engine (the type used in Spitfires). A day or two later a chance remark from another friend led to the whereabouts of a Gryphon engine, a marinised Merlin – close enough for the original enquirer who bought it and saved it from the scrapyard.

If all this seems rather wild, just stick to friends and relations. Family TV-watching-ing evenings are much the same regardless of the family, though the furnishings and choice of programme may differ. If you want a lawn-mowing shot, you probably have a neighbour who fits the image you need, and if you don't, you probably have a friend who lives in an area where the kind of lawn you want to photograph is usual.

With this kind of picture you have to

balance the probable returns against the certain cost. For example, jogging shots are often requested, and you may find it worthwhile to hire models for these. But indoor domestic scenes are more rarely requested, because many are specially shot, so a lower-cost picture with amateurs may be a better idea. There is however one domestic subject that is always in demand: children.

"Domestic" is a relative term; for some reason, we always find it much easier to march into the lives and homes of people abroad than to photograph people in our own culture — but the techniques required are the same no matter where you are.

Children

Pictures like this are quite common in black and white, but much harder to find (and to take!) in colour. Grainy, colourful, and busy, this photograph conveys the message that children play the same sort of games anywhere, but also that they always adapt to their surroundings, as here in Venice.

The market for pictures of children is very large indeed and runs from bathing and changing a baby (with the image suitably sanitised), through pictures of a tiny fist grabbing at a flower, children playing with dolls or toy soldiers, parties, first communions and bar mitzvahs, kite-flying, and rather self-conscious groups of adolescents leaning against the wall and shooting the breeze or sitting proudly on new motorcycles. Children at weddings, children at Christmas, children reading, children playing –

all sell again and again, for packaging, magazine illustrations, advertisements and countless other uses.

The best sellers are usually fairly young children – toddlers to around seven or eight years – who look spontaneous, healthy and lively, with casual clothes and tousled hair. On the other hand, there is a limit to the degree of realism that the market will accept; real dirt, real old clothes, and really untidy hair are simply not saleable. The children must conform to the

Children can be remarkably mobile subjects, and holding them in adequate focus is not always easy, as the picture of this relatively immobile young lady shows. There is an illusion of sharpness, because the plane of focus has captured her hair beautifully; but the loss of focus beyond that, and the unappealing expression, make this picture less saleable than it might otherwise be.

If a child's attention is captured, on the other hand, you can take your photographs at your leisure. Punch and Judy shows, fire-eaters, and all kinds of other entertainers can provide studies in concentration which every parent will immediately recognise.

stereotypes for childish appearance – round-cheeked and bright eyed, rather than pale and interesting. Next in popularity are babies, though they are so difficult to photograph that many of the pictures you see are of diminutive professionals, touted around the model agencies by their parents almost from birth. The market for adolescents is much smaller, but at this age the sale of pictures of girls tends to go up, a phenomenon that is confirmed by the success of David Hamilton's soft-core nymphettes.

Photographing children at different ages is such a difficult exercise if it is to be done well that there is little that can be said here. To begin with, the photographer must like (or at least not dislike) children. Except for special effects, all children of all ages look better if you come down to their eye level or below. This is not just a matter of the psychological implications of 'looking down on someone'; it also removes the risk of foreshortened bodies and heads that loom disporportionately large. Very small children need to have their mothers close at hand, and their attention (and elusive smiles) can usually be obtained with a noise of some kind – jingling a bunch of keys is very effective. Toddlers have such a short attention span that they seem to forget both the camera and the photographer after a while, but watch out for sticky little fingers. Always talk to children as seriously as you would to an adult; they have an acute ear for being patronised. Consider their feelings and their mood; just like adults children can be serious, humorous, argumentative, animated or tired, although they do not always conceal their feelings so well. Humorous pictures, whether intentional or not, can upset a child as much as they would an adult who is shown in a bad light.

For genuinely uninhibited pictures the children should be among familiar people and surroundings (playgroups are ideal), or they should be somewhere that the novelty of their surroundings will excite and intrigue them – on holiday, at the vet's, or at the zoo perhaps. Preferably they should also be doing something which interests them. The techniques for this sort of photography are rather like sports photography (though you do not need such long lenses), and the results can be excellent.

Characters

Every city and town has its 'characters', people who stand out from the crowd. Sometimes their conspicuousness is a result of personal eccentricity, like the man who used to frequent the King's Road in London wearing a Union Jack suit, looking like a rather thin John Bull. For others, their appearance is part of the job: think of an old-fashioned town crier, or the *Evzones* on guard duty in Greece. Some belong to a recognisable type, such as the Chelsea pensioner, the New York cop or the Texan urban cowboy. And then there are those who dress up for a special event, like the Up-Helly-Aa Vikings or the people at the Renaissance Fair at Agoura, near Los Angeles.

If the costumes are widely known, or colourful enough, they may be used as travel advertisements or on jigsaws. The Yeomen of the Guard might adorn a record cover, while posters of guardsmen on Horseguards Parade sell steadily as souvenirs. There is also editorial use: an Amish couple driving a horse-drawn trap to market might find a place in a general-interest magazine or even a textbook.

Some of these people accept that being photographed is a part of the job. Others have no strong feelings either way, but there is always the danger with eccentrics that they may have an irrational objection to being photographed, or demand large sums of money in return for having their picture taken. There was one London pavement artist, for example, who always flew into a violent rage when he was photographed. Incidentally, photographing such vanishing activities as pavement art has a value all of its own, as described on page 162.

Rollfilm is obviously best for taking saleable pictures of those who have no objection to being photographed, but for pictures that have to be taken 'on the wing' (New York cops, pavement artists and so forth) 35mm is more practical and is readily acceptable in most markets. A 90mm lens and a pair of running shoes may be the ideal kit for this activity; neither of the authors has ever been physically attacked, but we have been asked (sometimes abusively) for money, and on more than one occasion discretion has proved the better part of valour.

The most difficult problems are usually framing and metering. For the former, you need a clean and uncluttered background, perhaps with enough clear space for copy to be dropped in. Tight framing is only a partial answer, and often differential focus and a dark background will help enormously. For metering there may be a strong case for using one of the more sophisticated automatic systems, as their metering patterns are designed for precisely this sort of picture, but otherwise you need to take frequent incident light readings and to have an almost instinctive sense of what corrections to make for depth of shade, angle, and whether or not there is a cloud across the sun. Either way you are shooting for the percentages, and unless you are shooting a really easy subject (such as a well-lit and immobile guardsman), it may take half a roll of film to get precisely the effect that you want.

There are always more exhibitionists about than you might expect – and this patriotic punk makes an intriguing picture. Such subjects can be mercurial, and the photographer has to be prepared to be friendly, open, and quick on his feet, but most exhibitionists love to be photographed, almost by definition.

Market stallholders seem to be "characters" more often than not, and people like this lady are hard to resist as photographic subjects. It is difficult to tell what she is actually selling, which makes the shot particularly useful as it does not tie the subject matter down too much.

A medium-long lens – 90mm to 135mm on a 35mm camera – can be invaluable for picking out faces like this from a crowd. A zoom lens is tempting, but unfortunately there have been very few which could deliver the requisite quality.

127

Grab Shots

The amateur photographic magazines tell you that you should carry your camera at all times, because you never know what you will see. Although there is something to be said for such advice – it does a great deal to promote your level of visual awareness – the number of sale-able pictures that you will get is not that high. Even if you do spot a good subject, the odds are that it will have vanished or moved on before you get your camera ready. We all have pre-occupations that prevent us giving photography our full attention at all times, such as what we are going to have for dinner, what we can do about our tax demands, or what our chances are with the new secretary. Nevertheless, it is possible to go out looking for pictures, and to find them. Some people do it in their lunch hour; some do it at weekends; some do it in the evenings. It is not a good idea to look too often, because you can become stale or simply distracted. Lunch-hour pictures might include the pretzel-seller on the street corner, the road-sweeper, the elegantly-dressed lady looking in the jeweller's window, or the young secretaries on a park bench, eating their sandwiches. Evening pictures could be taken in bars or wherever else you go for relaxation (but do not get so relaxed that you lose your camera), and week-end shots might be of a rally, a fair, or a day at the seaside or zoo.

There are four things to watch out for in addition to the points already noted in the section on photographing 'characters' – where they are also relevant. The first is the weather. Accept that there are times when it is not worth shooting: it is usually easier to take pictures in sunshine, and it is almost always easier to sell them, though there are plenty of pictures to be had in snow or even driving rain. Wet streets at night can still look good, but don't just shoot for the sake of shooting. Secondly, there is the need to concentrate on the up-beat side of life. It is all too easy to concentrate on the negative side of things: the down-and-outs, the dustbins and extravagant trash of the consumer society, the cracked and peeling paint of old buildings. Such pictures might form the basis for an excellent magazine article, and they might win prizes at the local camera club, but they will not sell as well as pictures that stress the more attractive aspects of life. Thirdly, you need a keen eye for

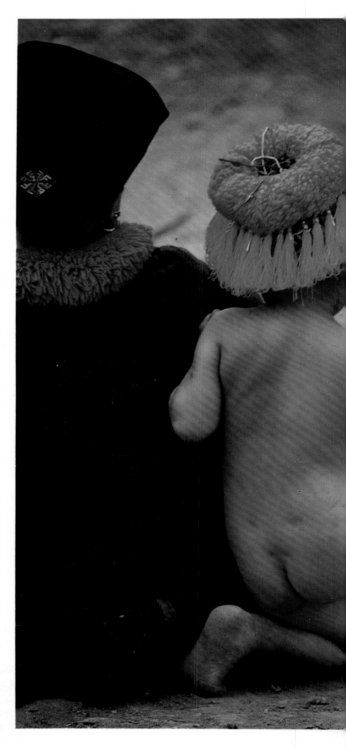

detail. Most city streets are littered, and litter will spoil many photographs. Obtrusive signs (particularly public lavatory signs, for some reason) can dominate a picture. And finally, many pictures may be marred by people or vehicles that come between you and your subject while the mirror of your reflex is up. This is why so many reportage photographers use Leicas, but you can always put a direct-vision finder in the accessory shoe of your SLR.

A picture which any parent would love to have of their child, and which therefore has a very wide appeal. In theory, you could set it up; in practice, the juxtaposition of the various elements is not something that most people would readily imagine.

The standard advice on zoo photography is to use a wide aperture and try to lose the bars; but here, the very human expression of the subject ties in well with his bars, and he becomes a metaphor for all the people who are trapped in dead-end jobs. A visit to the zoo is often the inspiration for a lot of pictures, though the temptation to overshoot is very strong.

Reportage and Industrial

Historically, reportage pictures were grainy, black-and-white slice-of-life photographs in the tradition of Weegee's *Naked City*, while industrial pictures were major set pieces, showing off 'major advances in industry' in a suitably heroic fashion. There is still room for both approaches today, but to a surprising extent the two fields have moved together and now share a lot of common ground.

For feature reportage (as distinct from 'hard news'), pictures are now as likely to be in colour as in black and white. Technical quality has improved immensely, although the old badly exposed (and even more badly printed) monochromes survive to this day, as can be seen from the display outside the average newspaper office. There is still a demand for really impressive large format pictures of oil refineries and new factories, and the demand for shots of factories glowing in the setting sun, or set off by a sheet of water or in a rural setting, is as great as it ever was. But gradually industrial photography is

concentrating more on the role of people in industry.

From the point of view of stock photography, the primary concern is likely to be emotional rather than narrative, even though both reportage and industrial photography are in the nature of things likely to tell more of a story than, say, a pin-up picture or a tourist-board landscape. The straightforward 'how-to' picture is likely to find much less of a market than the 'what it is like' picture, whether 'what it is like' is good or bad.

The two fields have also moved closer together in the realm of equipment. The old reporter used a Speed Graphic with a five-inch lens and on-camera flash every time, and the industrial photographer used a half-plate, whole-plate or even 10 x 8″ view camera, utilising the movements for almost every picture; nowadays both are likely to get more use from the 35mm camera, whether SLR or Leica rangefinder. Fast handling, light weight, a wide range of lenses, infrequent reloading, and the low cost of film

"Dark satanic mills" almost always look more dramatic (and a good deal more satanic) when accompanied by billowing smoke and steam. Often, different processes are run at different times of day, which means that you have to find out when there will be the most atmospheric discharge. Certain atmospheric conditions also accentuate the effect: a humid day with a very gentle breeze is usually best. Intriguingly, pictures like this were once regarded as evidence of successful industry; nowadays, a factory owner would probably be appalled at such a shot.

allow 'shooting around' the subject to create a picture story. Increasingly, the picture story is in demand for company reports, instead of the older, more static style of photography. As a general rule, medium format cameras have not the speed of handling needed for a picture story. Neither do they have the image quality, nor (more importantly) the camera movements required for set pieces, though a few industrial photographers do swear by the 6 x 7cm Baby Linhof for both kinds of work, and acquit themselves very well.

Once again, the primary use of both industrial and reportage photographs is likely to be something other than stock photography. However, special shoots can be worth arranging just for stock, because this gives more scope for experiment – something that might not be available on a commissioned shoot. The additional revenue obtained from editorial, encyclopaedia and textbook, leaflet, brochure and other use can be quite considerable.

A characteristic of industrial design is often the use of bold, simple shapes. This massive cooling tower, with an electricity pylon in the background, says a great deal about the way in which man has used and abused the countryside.

The dramatic effect of a mass of smoke can also be emphasised by showing it against a clear, deep blue sky, or (as here) by creating a composition combining backlighting and silhouette.

There are some photographers who make a virtue out of being noticed, and thus produce posed pictures in the style of a hundred years ago. Although there is something to be said for this approach, there is no doubt that the modern style is to be as unobtrusive as possible, and to photograph people going about their daily work as if there were no photographer present.

For this reason, flash needs to be handled with caution. There is certainly a place for carefully lit pictures (usually with three heads, though two can be used at a pinch), and for fill-in flash, but on-camera flash often looks unnatural, as well as limiting the speed at which you can work to the recycling time of the flashgun. Any flash also advertises your presence in a way which you may not want, and in industrial situations the momentary blinding caused by the flash can be very dangerous.

The trinity of fast film, fast lenses, and long exposures also has its drawbacks. Fast films are obviously grainier than slow ones, but if you

This picture conveys many things about factory life. The massive pressings are in the foreground, and their shape is repeated oppressively. The enormous stamping machine still further diminishes the figure who is working it, and the inevitable question arises: who is master, man or machine?

With set-up pictures like this one, you must be careful that you do not produce a result which is incongruous or even laughable to anyone who knows the subject. Why is the subject tracing a circuit with a soldering iron? And why is the soldering iron pointing at what appears to be a resistor, when D3 in the circuit is clearly a transistor or other diode? Your subject can normally help you to avoid the worst gaffes.

decide to go to 120 for better image quality, you are usually limited to f/2.8 standard lenses, and even slower if you want wide-angles or long focus. An additional consideration is the smaller depth of field of rollfilm lenses, which is an inescapable mathematical consequence of the increased size of the image. It can be very difficult trying to decide whether you will get better quality by using Kodachrome 64 and a 35mm f/1.4 Nikkor or Summilux (the only two usable 35mm f/1.4 lenses), or 400 ASA rollfilm

pushed to 650 ASA and a 53mm f/4.5 Biogon. It is true that there are a few fast lenses for 120 cameras, notably Mamiya's 80mm f/1.9 for the M645 and the 110mm f/2 for the Hasselblad, but they are expensive and heavy when compared with the slower versions, and depth of field can be negligible. The massive 150mm f/2.8 Xenotars for 5 x 4″ are even more specialised.

For action, 35mm is the only realistic choice in most cases, with wide-angle lenses taking the lead. Indoors, you may need a wide-angle to get everything in, and out of doors, the advantage of a wide angle is that you can get in front of obstructions rather than having them in front of you. You also need speed in most cases, which is one of the reasons why the Leica still has a significant share of the market among reportage photographers: their 21mm f/2.8, 35mm f/1.4, 50mm f/1, 75mm f/1.4, and 90mm f/2 optics are probably the best available at (or near) those focal lengths, and the 50/1 has no competitors at all in current production. They are also smaller, lighter, simpler, quieter, and easier to focus in poor light than reflexes, though most Leica users also keep an old Nikon F or something similar for lenses longer than 90mm.

For static shots, longer exposures are possible; also larger formats, slower films and smaller apertures, but you can then run into reciprocity failure problems which require not only additional exposure, but also filtration to correct colour shifts. Some colour shifts, however, can actually work to your advantage, giving beautiful and surreal hues to otherwise ordinary subjects.

This somewhat Dali-esque vision of quality control is unlikely to be a very successful stock picture, because it is tied too closely to the painting of box-like metal enclosures; by concentrating more strongly on the man with the clipboard, a picture of more universal applicability could have been created.

Researching the Subject

Even more than for most kinds of photography, it pays to do your homework before you ever consider taking industrial or reportage photographs. This will not only give you a clear idea of the main things that you want to shoot: it will also enable you to judge the relative importance of subjects that may be visually exciting and may prove suitable for stock photography, but which are strictly peripheral to the main subject. It also reduces the likelihood of embarrassing yourself by asking stupid questions. For this reason, it is also worth finding out the names of the key people in that particular firm or establishment.

Once you have found out all that you can about the subject, make out a shot list, drawing on both your intellectual appreciation of the

People's homes can often furnish attractive ''filler'' pictures for a photojournalisatic essay; they can show how the lifestyle is all of a piece, or they can be used to draw a contrast between (say) an electronic engineer's high-technology occupation and his centuries-old house.

subject and any particularly eye-catching images that you may have encountered during your research, or remember from the past. When you actually see the subject it may not be at all as you imagined it; a ship's engine room, for example, looks more like a power generating station than the sort of engine room that most people picture from the days of steam reciprocating engines. In some cases, there may be nothing that you can do about this, but you may be able to use ultra-wide lenses, dramatic lighting, juxtaposition with something else or a special effects filter to liven up dull pictures. In other cases, you may be able to find a real Victorian engine room that will provide a good stock shot (people always like to have their preconceptions confirmed). In any case, it is well worth having the list of possible shots, as it helps you to work out a framework for the shoot.

Ideally you should be reasonably familiar with your subject from past experience; a photojournalist will often spend what seems to be an incredibly long time covering a single story, because he knows that each time he goes back he will meet more people and learn a little more from them, so that better pictures are possible. At the very least you should walk through the factory or town or whatever it is that you are going to cover, preferably a few days before the shoot itself, so that you can let the images sort themselves out in your head, and plan a logical shooting sequence. It is a good idea to go through your prepared shot list with your contact, adding some ideas and deleting others, if at all possible. This can result in valuable extra ideas, and often has the additional result that because you have involved someone 'on the inside' he takes much more of a personal interest in the subject and really goes out of his way to help you. At every stage, try to verbalise why you are taking the pictures, what you want, and how you are going to express it, including any special techniques you are using, such as zooming during exposure, panning, grain and special effects filters. It is all very well to say that the creative process is non-verbal, but unless you do this, it is all to easy to flounder around and end up with a set of pictures which are at best disconnected, and at worst simply bad.

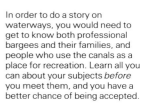

In order to do a story on waterways, you would need to get to know both professional bargees and their families, and people who use the canals as a place for recreation. Learn all you can about your subjects *before* you meet them, and you have a better chance of being accepted.

Dealing with People

In reportage and industrial photography you are more than usually dependent on the goodwill of other people to help you get the pictures that you want. In many cases, you will need permission to go in and take the pictures in the first place. Once you have got that, you need someone to guide you around and tell you what is going on, and then you need the cooperation (or at least non-obstruction) of other senior people. Finally, you need the cooperation of your subjects; only a very few pictures can be taken without the subjects being aware of it. As a general rule you will find that personality is a better key to the best and most saleable pictures than technique.

The initial contact must be made at as high a level as possible, in order to ensure that permission is not later revoked. It should also be made in such a way that those in less senior positions are not offended. In other words, you need to 'go through the proper channels', but it is also a good idea to approach two or three 'proper channels' simultaneously. This need not be more than a letter to the Managing Director, a letter to the Factory Manager, and a letter to the Marketing, Publicity or PR managers, stating the same basic facts and making the same requests in each case, and letting each of them know that you have written to the other two. This approach reduces to a minimum the risk of anyone feeling that he should have been consulted, but was not, and the further risk that the letter will simply be ignored. It also means that you may have not one but three valuable sources of information and ideas. Even on a commissioned shoot, you should always insist on being introduced to all the people who can help you, preferably well before the shoot itself.

Explain in your letter that you sell stock pictures, that as their company is a well-known (or successful or particularly good) example, you automatically thought of them, and that although you cannnot guarantee anything it is unlikely that the publicity will do them anything but good. Do not necessarily offer pictures at this stage, as they will probably ask for them anyway; when they do, tell them that you will be delighted to supply copies of the best, cost-free. Give them repro quality dupes, but not too many. Strike a balance between the benefit to you and the benefit to them (the free pictures); if you give them too many you may be cutting your own throat, because a few really good free pictures may lead to further commissions, whereas too many free photographs may mean that they come to expect you to work for nothing in return for the privilege of photographing them. It may be possible to build up a long-term relationship with the people in question, which usually means that as you get to know them better, you are granted better access and therefore have the chance to take better pictures. In addition to this, you will be the person they automatically think of for commissioned work. This has certainly been the case for one of the authors, whose commitment to the Tibetan cause must by now be quite obvious.

Once you get on to the shop floor, or out into the villages, or on board the ship, you will need a minder to help you. He (or she) will assist you in getting the best pictures with the minimum of disruption and the minimum of risk to yourself and others. This invaluable assistant can steer you away from those parts of town where they would steal your cameras, or advise you against stepping over loose hawsers without first ascertaining exactly where the two ends are, or stop you inadvertently endangering others by putting your tripod and power cables in the wrong place. Your minder should also enjoy some status, but not be a symbol of unwanted authority. In a factory, a foreman or well-liked manager is the most useful; other situations will have other minders. In a small organisation, your contact may well be the boss himself, which can be extremely useful as he will know the set-up intimately and will have no problems with areas that are off-limits, except perhaps the reactor room or the operating theatre at prime time.

As for the people you actually photograph, you can try to catch them unawares to begin with (if this is not too dangerous, either to you or to them), or you can be introduced (or introduce yourself) and then try either posing them or asking them to get on with their business and ignore you. One of the authors finds that most people (especially his employees) tend to do the last almost automatically. Each of the three approaches has its place, but the 'unposed' pose tends to be more difficult than just asking to be ignored. Your minder should stick with you

There are ethical questions in a picture like this; the monk is almost certainly breaking his vows, and you should ask yourself whether the amusement value of the picture warrants showing him in a bad light. The authors' view is that it, because (as a good Buddhist) he ought to accept what is, even while striving for what is not. At least he is unlikely to get nasty about it, because Buddhist monks are famed for their renunciation of violence!

"Sahib . . . sahib . . . you give money, sahib?" All too often, a picture of a colourful local like this can degenerate into a squabble if you are in a tourist area; but where you are dealing with unspoiled and genuine people, as here, your subject is often delighted to have his picture taken.

Photographing children is a minefield in its own right, though the worst countries are paradoxically those of the developed West; in America and England, anyone who wants to photograph little boys and girls is often credited with the worst of motives.

and ensure that you do not breach safety regulations, which occur in almost every factory. Lack of attention to such rules can result in an excellent shot being scrapped after it has been taken; one of the authors recalls a dramatic picture of a high mast which could not be used because the men at the top were not wearing the required safety harness. It is useful to have informed comment on the pictures from your contacts, but never allow them the right of veto

if you can possibly help it.

If someone genuinely does not want to be photographed, respect their wishes; it is very rare indeed that you will have to steal a picture or go without. More often the problem is that people want prints for themselves. Although taking pictures of all and sundry can be expensive and time-consuming, the easiest course is probably to have a spare camera body loaded with colour negative film, which you can have

The danger with photographing girls that you do not know on the beach is that they (or worse, their boyfriends/husbands/fathers) may assume that you have ulterior motives. If there is obviously a male companion around, placate him before you take the picture.

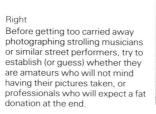

Right
Before getting too carried away photographing strolling musicians or similar street performers, try to establish (or guess) whether they are amateurs who will not mind having their pictures taken, or professionals who will expect a fat donation at the end.

developed and printed at very low cost and then send in its entirety (negs and all) to your minder, with a covering letter. The alternative, duping transparencies on to neg stock, is even more expensive and time consuming and easier to forget. Polaroid pictures at the time are very convenient, but can also be very expensive and time consuming. Sending pictures is a sure way of being remembered with affection, and can be invaluable if you return to the same place.

Above
Once, a stock photograph was used to illustrate the crowds at a well-known beach. Unfortunately, it showed a young man with a former girl-friend, and his wife saw the picture. His protestations that it had been taken two or three years previously fell on deaf ears, and eventually he had to sue to clear his name with his wife.

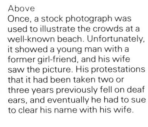

Morris dancers, and others who perform in public as a hobby rather than as a means of earning a living, are normally perfectly happy to be photographed. Buy them a beer and they become even happier; if you want to cause a little innocent havoc, buy them lots of beer and see if you can get them happy enough to fall over each other while dancing.

Set Pieces

Set pieces are not confined to new factories, new machines and the like; they can also include group pictures – the sort of carefully constructed image that shows a 'hive of activity', with people all working away at different tasks, giving the impression of a harmonious and co-operative whole.

Since the nature of the set piece is that it is detailed and carefully set up, it is reasonable to use at least a rollfilm camera, and preferably 5x4″. In the case of many architectural shots, the rising front may be all but essential. There are also some pictures which will require tilts and swings: an interior picture of a new lobby may require all the camera movements you can muster. Extreme wide angles can also be very useful, and Hasselblad's superb SWC/M, with its 38mm f/4.5 Biogon, is exceptional.

The sort of set piece that is required by stock picture buyers will normally be very general – a picture of a refinery, some factory chimneys, or a factory interior, and in many cases (such as a man operating a lathe) they may be content with 35mm, depending on the intended use. Take the example of a refinery, because it is a subject which can be particularly photogenic if it is treated well and singularly dull if it is not, the *modus operandi* can be broken down into a number of simple steps.

First, there is the question of viewpoint. Can you get the viewpoint that you have in your mind's eye? Could you get it if you stood on a stepladder, or on top of a car, or do you need an aerial picture? Could you use a long-focus lens and go further away? The time-honoured device of a pair of black card L-shapes can help you determine both viewpoint and lens required, without imposing the limitations that checking through the viewfinder can bring. But if you do use the viewfinder, try stopping down and looking at the darkened image: it often helps you to see the shapes more easily, and composition is mainly a matter of the arrangement of shapes.

Secondly, how much do you need to show? Could you use a detail to say all that was needed? One of the characteristics of a refinery is flaming off waste; could you capture the flame-off, with just enough surroundings to give it context?

Thirdly, what about lighting and weather? A deep blue sky is usually best, but there are

This is not a set piece on the grand scale, but it was very carefully set up, as can be seen from the lighting. If you know that you want a picture of a welder (or anything similar), try to give as much advance warning as possible; all too often, you are told, "Oh, Bert was doing that just this morning. It would have been a marvellous picture – but he's just finished . . ."

The fish-eye lens rarely has a place in reportage work, and although the characteristic distortion here conveys something of the brassiness and gaudiness of the occasion, most people would not find this image either attractive or informative.

This apparently artless photograph is actually a carefully contrived set piece. Dry-stone walls, wooden gates, sheep, and men who look like the grizzled farmers that they are, do not come together by accident. Scouting the factory or farm for locations which convey the feeling you want is usually essential, before you ever attempt to take a "set piece" picture.

occasions when that is simply not available. Or you may actually prefer a flat white sky and flat white lighting as a foil to effects filters: the various graduated types, especially the sunset graduated, can produce results that are widely appreciated by buyers. For a straight picture, the best time of day would probably be early dusk, when there is still enough light to show the intricacies of the pipework but the sky is dark enough to show the flame-off to maximum advantage. For an unusual effect, a soft-focus lens might be tried; refineries are not usually thought of as romantic places, but there is a certain magic about them, which this could convey.

Chapter 8

STOCK IN THE STUDIO

Introduction

'Studio' is a very flexible term. It can mean anything from a fully-equipped professional studio, with coves, racks of background paper, and 10,000 watt-seconds of electronic flash, to a temporarily adapted living room with a couple of photofloods and some home-made reflectors. 'Studio stock shots' are much easier to define, in form if not in content. They are carefully planned and lit, and superbly executed. The subjects are mostly of the chocolate-box variety – flowers, still lifes, animals. Stock shots of people have been covered in Chapter 7.

There is another side to stock in the studio, which is dealt with at the end of this chapter. It is concerned with the after-work and special effects that can be achieved in the studio, such as double exposures and sandwiched slides, montage, and special processing for grain, contrast, etc.

The professional with a fully equipped studio inevitably has a much wider scope for studio stock shots than the amateur. For example, he may be able to handle cars, large animals, and (if his studio is appropriately equipped) food photography; few amateurs are likely to be able to fit a Ferrari or a horse into their living rooms, despite bland assurances in the amateur photographic press that 'you can achieve professional results in an easily converted corner…etc.' Food photography is a very strange discipline, usually involving specialised cooks who are as skilled in making food look good as in making it taste good. It may also rely on various *ersatz* materials, such as shaving cream for whipped cream, cigarette smoke for steam, and a coating of glycerine for an attractive gloss. The professional may also be able to shoot stock pictures on the back of a commissioned shoot, and if he knows an aspiring food preparation expert (the title 'cook' is quite inadequate), he may be able to arrange portfolio shots to their mutual advantage.

Both car and food photography are expensive undertakings, and there is probably less demand for studio pictures than for pictures of cars out of doors or of food in a location setting (for example, at a beautifully prepared hotel buffet). Most 'chocolate box' animal pictures can be taken just as well by an amateur with a temporary studio as by a professional who uses a couple of unbooked days for stock photography, though the professional will probably be able to do it more easily and with less domestic disruption. Puppies and kittens may look cute, but they do have their disadvantages, unless they are house-trained.

There is very little chance of selling studio shots unless they are on rollfilm or large format film: 35mm is unlikely even to be considered by most buyers, and even if it is duped up to a larger size, the pictures are unlikely to have the biting sharpness that is usually associated with this sort of photography – though there are of course occasions when moody shots will sell, just as with any other sort of photography. Finally, there are few, if any, photographers who make a full-time living at studio stock photography. As already mentioned, it is a matter of a professional turning some spare studio time to advantage, or the amateur earning some useful extra income.

Food shots are a speciality in themselves, but one for which there is a constant demand. Large format pictures are the norm, but sometimes rollfilm is used: the lower picture on this page was shot on a 645 camera.

Flowers

As with other types of studio photography, flower shots are deceptively difficult. Finding perfect blooms in their prime is not easy; just look at your local florist's stock. Obviously, most florists are unwilling to let you pick and choose, so the only answer in most cases is to buy many more flowers than you need, perhaps several times as many, and select the best. You could also consider going to the early-morning flower market, where the florists buy. You will have to buy a lot of flowers, but prices will be far lower, and the flowers will be very fresh.

Secondly, you need a photogenic vase or jug, or preferably a selection of containers. A robust bunch of country flowers might sit best in an earthenware jug, whereas a single rose would look better in a tall, elegant Scandinavian glass vase.

Thirdly, you will need a flower arranger, unless you are confident of your own ability. Professional flower arrangers do exist, but they are alarmingly expensive, and unless you can find one who needs some pictures for her portfolio you may prefer to use an amateur. Even then, you have to allow for personal taste; one of the authors sometimes works with an arranger who trained at the Sogetsu school in Tokyo; an arrangement based on hundreds of years of Japanese tradition may not suit an English chocolate box.

Fourthly, it is almost essential to have a choice of backgrounds: light, dark, matching, contrasting, patterned, plain, and preferably transilluminated as well. Supports for the vase may include plate glass, plain wood (in various colours), and perhaps a chequered gingham tablecloth; the variations are innumerable. Light-

ing should be by electronic flash, because the heat of tungsten will soon cause flowers to wilt and droop. A very useful accessory is a perfume atomiser filled with water; this not only helps to reduce wilting, but also creates a 'dew fresh' look to be created artificially.

Finally, it is worth noting that the colours of some of the paler flowers do not record on film in quite the way that you would expect, because of the ultra-violet and infra-red which the petals reflect. Filtration for this can be impossible, and in cases of difficulty the safe guide is that colour balance is not critical – as long as it is warm. You may find that a warming filter (81-series, CCO5R, or R1) is as useful in flower photography as in taking pin-up pictures.

For the shoot itself you will usually need to work both fast and delicately if you want to catch the flowers at their best; even a few hours can make them look tired, and rough handling will make them dog-eared very quickly indeed. Photograph the arrangement both with and without the vase in shot, and consider close-ups, differential focus, directional lighting, and possibly effects filters for striking pictures.

Delicate wild flowers – and daisies are surprisingly delicate – almost invariably look best in their natural habitat. In many countries, it may also be illegal to pick or dig up the rare species.

These ''catalogue shots'' of
flowers have little merit other than
as accurate records of a particular
flower's appearance – but this is
exactly what a seedsman might
want for a seed catalogue or
packet.

Still Life

Still-life photographs can be very lucrative, as well as extremely instructive. They are merciless in their exposure of faulty technique, but there is considerable satisfaction in doing one well. The difficulties may best be illustrated by taking an example: a still life with two or three old leather-bound books, a candle and a pair of old-fashioned, gold-rimmed half-moon spectacles.

In the largest cities – London, New York, Los Angeles – there are prop agencies who can supply an immense range of props, at a price. One of the authors recalls being dispatched, as an assistant, to order 30 goatskin rugs which were delivered from stock without demur. There are occasions when it is worth spending money at a commercial prop agency, or when props that have been hired for a particular commissioned shoot can be used to create a stock shot, but unless you have access to a prop agency, you will have to get your props somewhere else. The traditional approach is of course to send your assistant out with a modest sum from the petty cash and instructions not to return until he has got what is needed – assistants read on!

The main sources, apart form hiring, are buying, borrowing and bodging. Some photographers keep stocks of commonly used props, and even buy promising-looking inexpensive props on the off-chance that they might come in handy. For the shot described above, an old chenille curtain or tablecloth might already be in stock; candles can be bought easily. The problems are the candle-holder, the books, and the glasses.

Books might be borrowed from a friend, or from an antiquarian bookstore. If you use the latter you may have to pay a deposit of the full value, sometimes with a modest hire fee, though surprisingly, many places are willing to lend things for nothing, especially if there is any chance of their being credited somewhere. You would need to pay particular attention to the titles of the books – a point easily overlooked when you see a fine binding. The candle-holder is more difficult. A new one is out of the question, as it will look distinctly second-hand if any wax is dripped on it, and the same objection may (or may not) apply to an antique one. The best bet is either to buy a good second-hand one, or borrow one from a friend who actually uses it. Finally, the glasses might be borrowed from

an optician or an antique store; there is little risk of their being damaged, so you do not have to worry too much.

In this particular shot, you might only require a little bodging: the books might be placed over the moth-holes in the chenille, for example. In other pictures the pieces of modelling putty, matchsticks, and carefully chosen angles are what make the difference between a beautiful illusion and a complete mess. There are also

Not all still lifes are food shots, but it is certainly true that these are one of the best-selling types. The best shots to begin with are the ones which do not require skilled professional help, such as the coffee shot on this spread, or the classic arrays of raw ingredients and culinary equipment, but even home-prepared Cornish mussels can be made to look professional if properly photographed.

professional bodges, such as dabbing bright metal with putty (or using a dulling spray, or putting it in a refrigerator so that condensation forms on the surface when it is taken out) to kill reflections; it is a field in which you can learn a great deal. Finally, the lighting must be very carefully done if it is not to overwhelm the candlelight, and if the yellow light of the candle (colour temperature about 1800 K) is to play an important part in the mood of the picture.

Animals

The surprisingly high prices that pictures of kittens and puppies can command indicate two things: the level of demand and the difficulty of supply.

Models can come from a number of sources. There are hire agencies for animals, just as for props, or you can approach breeders, cat or dog boarding kennels, or simply rely on friends. With cats, fluffy long-haired kittens generally sell well, along with Siamese and other exotic short-hairs, but there is also a demand for well-groomed adult cats of indeterminate origin; pet food manufacturers – a good market – do not want their products to look too snobbish. With dogs, the different breeds each have their own different characteristics – the alertness of a German Shepherd, the soulful look of a bloodhound – which the photograph should bring out. Among other small animals, parrots are quite widely sought after, and there is a certain demand for hamsters, mice, guineapigs, chicks and snakes.

Most successful animal photographers are specialists who get to know the ways of the animals they photograph. For example, if you feed a cat, it will wash when it has finished eating; go to sleep; wake up and stretch; perhaps yawn; and then be ready to be placed in a position for posed shots. All you need to do for feeding, sleeping, and stretching pictures, therefore, is to provide comfortable, photogenic, well-lit surroundings. For the posed pictures, you will need to have the props ready and lit (and perhaps Polaroid-tested with a soft toy standing in for the animal). For some shots, you may be able to short-circuit matters by (for example) smearing a little bacon grease on a cat's whiskers; this will almost invariably start the animal washing.

Chimpanzees are one of the less readily available animals, but there is a fair demand for pictures, and a picture like this need not be hard to arrange.

There is a tremendous market for pictures of cats of all kinds, for advertising, packaging, and even editorial use. The two shots above are typical of the very high quality which is expected as a matter of course, but the lower picture shows a rather different aspect of feline life, which may still prove saleable and which will certainly face less competition.

It is as well to limit the range of movement of the animal, by setting up the posed pictures on a table-top or chair. Photographers who specialise in animal shots often have a purpose-built stand with a top about a foot square, mounted on a swivel so that it can be revolved as necessary. An assistant to move the stand and replace the animal is indispensible; if you are photographing more than one animal, it is as well to have more than one assistant. The assistant can also use a whistle or clear-toned bell to attract the animal's attention, though this must not be done too often or it will cease to work. No matter how much you may be tempted, it is never worth sedating an animal; not only is it cruelty to dumb animals, but the animal will look sedated in the picture.

There are technical problems too. Focusing must be spot-on or fur will look indistinct, and because fur 'eats' light it is usually necessary to give a stop or so more exposure than is indicated by an incident-light meter. Carefully snooted lights are almost essential, and a dark-toned background is useful. Because you are dealing with split-second poses and expressions, it is as well to use the camera on a tripod and pre-focus, setting an aperture which allows depth of field to take care of subject movement. For close-ups, move the whole camera rather than trying to focus. The delay between pressing the shutter release and making the exposure can also be critical: the 1/60 second delay of a Rollei TLR or Linhof rangefinder camera makes life much easier than the 1/10 second or so of the average rollfilm SLR. Finally, you have to shoot for the percentages; it is by no means unusual to expose three, four, or more rolls of 120 to get a single saleable picture.

In the Workroom

Double exposure is one of the most useful workroom techniques for adding interest or drama to a picture. Moon, sun, sky and firework pictures can be used to add interest to dull skies, and it is possible to create many surreal and dramatic pictures using the same techniques.

Technically, double exposures are relatively simple; any camera with a double-exposure capability can be used, though it must be rigidly mounted or it may move when the shutter is re-cocked for the second exposure. Rollfilm is preferable, both to help preserve quality (you are adding an extra generation to the photographic process) and because it is easier to mark the ground-glass screen (or use an overlay) to ensure precise registration. The copying lens must also be able to deliver first-class quality at the appropriate image distances; many people use an enlarger lens rather than a camera lens for this reason. The light source must be a known quantity, either constant (as in an Illumi-tran or similar electronic flash copier) or controllable, as with a dichroic tungsten copier. The main technical problems are associated with exposure determination, colour balance, and contrast control. The first two are a matter for experiment, and the third can be adjusted by choice of film stock (including low-contrast duplicating film) and varying processing time, as described in Chapter 5. You must also pay attention to the maximum density of your originals and of your copies: two blacks may not make a white, but two insufficiently dense blacks, plus slight over-exposure, may make a very unpleasant dark green. You can also make double exposures by projection in an enlarger, using a rollfilm back or even a 5 x 4″ cut-film holder on the enlarger baseboard. Because it is only in the darker areas of the one transparency that the lighter areas of the other will register, the best pictures for double exposure normally contain relatively large areas of darkness, even blackness. If the images are to overlap, so that the darker parts of one are seen through the lighter parts of the other, then the technique needed is sandwiching.

Sandwiching is exactly what its name suggests – putting two transparencies together and photographing the sandwich. It is often used to put a dramatic sky, or another background, behind a clearly recognisable silhouette – the Taj Mahal,

perhaps, or the Manhattan skyline – which may itself be derived from a black-and-white picture, or via a line negative. Some people seem to have an eye for sandwiches, with flowers-plus-girls being a favourite subject, but these 'creative' sandwiches are often more successful in competitions and photographic magazines than in the market place, where they need to be very well done and genuinely original if they are not to be dismissed as clichés.

Effects filters of all kinds can be used at the duplicating stage, often with more control than would be possible at the taking stage, though the effects are not always exactly the same as they would be if the filter had been used at the time of taking the picture. This can be an excellent way of giving new life to transparencies that did not quite make it. However, there are two things to remember: one is that some pictures cannot be saved no matter what you do to them, and the other is that it is easy to be carried away by technical ingenuity, sometimes to the detriment of visual effect.

Montage and **artwork** are much more difficult than any of the techniques already mentioned,

but they can be very effective. Montages are usually made from very high-quality colour prints, carefully cut out with a scalpel, and with the edges feathered with sandpaper before assembling the composite image with rubber solution. The joins may then be retouched, usually with an airbrush, before the picture is rephotographed on to transparency film. Airbrushed artwork, in the hands of a skilled artist, is almost indistinguishable from a photographic image; all sorts of weird and wonderful effects can be achieved, either directly on a photographic print or by montage.

It is usual to work on a scale two or three times larger than the final image that will be used when making montages or producing artwork, so that any flaws and errors are reduced when the final image is reproduced, rather than being magnified. With stock photography, where the final reproduction size is not known, the best approach is probably to work as large as possible, at least with a 14 x 11″ print and preferably with a 20 x 16″ . The Final transparency is usually made on 5 x 4″ film, or even larger. The cost of producing such pictures is so high that

Properly used, double exposure is a powerful creative tool, as witness the surrealistic picture of a red bird among looming towers. The danger, however, lies is using it in an attempt to save a failed picture by fair means or foul: restraint, and an eye for the dramatic rather than the merely unusual (or clichéd) are essential.

the extra cost of the film is negligible. Because of the cost involved, they would normally only be produced as a commission or as portfolio or promotional pictures for the photographer or artist.

Special processing techniques of various kinds can be used to increase or reduce contrast on original films, as described in Chapter 5, but it is generally safer to work with duplicates if special effects are wanted: for instance, it is easy to add grain in duplicating a Kodachrome original, whereas smoothing out graininess while retaining maximum image sharpness requires millions of dollars' worth of NASA image enhancement equipment. Instead of the processing techniques for increasing grain described in Chapter 5, it is also quite possible to magnify small portions of the original image while duplicating. Rather than using bellows and extremely long exposures, projection printing may again be the best approach.

By enlarging a 35mm shot on to 4 x 5in film, and some rather ingenious processing, this picture was given a fascinating 'hand-painted' look. This is the one section of the book where the authors really cannot 'tell all', because some of these techniques are experimental and hard to reproduce.

The photographer was unwilling to disclose details of how this dramatic effect was obtained, but it was almost certainly a striking original picture with the red sky-effects double-exposed in.

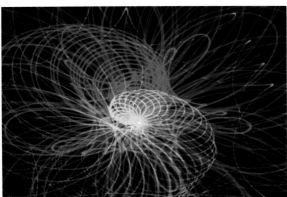

Five seconds at f/4 produced this swirl of laser light; similar effects can be obtained, with longer exposures, by fixing a torch to a pendulum or harmonograph.

Chapter 9

SPECIALIST SUBJECTS

The Specialist Market

There are libraries that specialise in particular subjects, such as wildlife, sport, aerial photographs, underwater pictures, or dance, and several major libraries have extensive specialist sub-collections which may actually be larger than the entire stock of some of the smaller specialist libraries. The whereabouts of special collections can be determined via special-interest magazines, or in Britain through BAPLA, the British Association of Picture Libraries and Agencies; similar bodies exist in several other countries. Fotobank uses a picture source computerised system, from which any collection can be listed. Besides a supplied list of photography sources, the researcher may enter their own contacts. Fast keyword searches enable any subject or location to be linked to a supplier.

Many people who take specialist pictures do it purely for love, with no thought of profit, or else build up a library as a side-effect of somethin´

else, be it academic research or freelance journalism. Often, specialist subjects will only show a financial profit if the pictures are first used to illustrate something else – a book or magazine article or whatever – and are then put into the library to earn extra revenue. Having said that, there is a surprisingly high demand for specialist pictures (notably wildlife and sport) and if a book, television programme, or part-work buys your pictures, they will often require a fair number.

There are three options when it comes to selling specialist pictures. The first is to run your own small library. This can be hard work, and you are unlikely to make a great deal of money unless you also handle the work of other photographers or broaden your range of subjects, or both, but many specialist libraries are run on this basis. If you are very specialised, you can become well known in your own small field, and

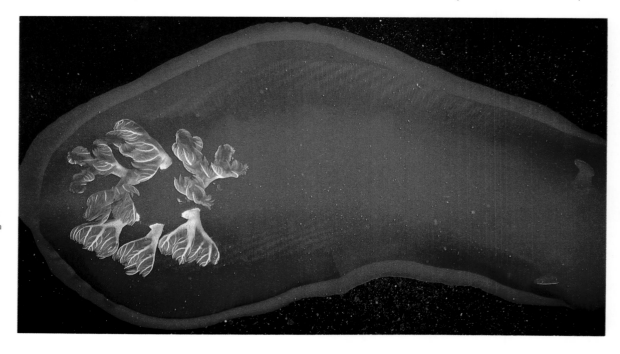

Often, scientific photographs will be all but meaningless except to a few specialists – but those specialists will immediately spot any errors of captioning, or even incongruities in the picture. Anyone running a library must insist that pictures are accurately captioned by the photographer; how many other people could caption a picture like this adequately?

do quite well. The second option is to place your pictures with a library already known for your speciality, and the third is to place them with a more general library. The advantages of the last are that they may try harder to sell your pictures, and that there may be no competition within the library. The decision between a specialist and a general library is not easy to make, and will depend on your knowledge of the market and your appreciation of the libraries involved.

As a rule, the best specialist pictures are taken by people who photograph only what interests them. This is not, by and large, a happy hunting ground for the general photographer. You have to be careful not to be too close to your subject, and you have to remember that not everyone shares your passion for, say, archaeology or Tibet. Unless your pictures are striking, or at least informative, they are unlikely to have any appeal at all outside the world of *afficionados*. The more specialised your subject is, the more likely this is to be true.

Hungry chicks are an image which is demanded surprisingly often, but you must be sure that they are not of an endangered or listed species; if they are, it may be illegal even to photograph them, to say nothing of the ecological damage you may unwittingly do.

Aerial photographs are always in demand, but they *must* be accurately captioned – something which can be a good deal more difficult than it sounds if you do not know the area yourself, and try to relate symbols on the map to images on the film.

Sport

Sports photography is the classic example of the readily saleable specialist subject. A few sports photographers discover their *forte* in a blinding flash of inspiration, but most begin with a genuine interest in the sport itself, and gradually work their way up from shooting obscure amateur events to shooting serious professional sport. Along the way, they refine their techniques and their choice of equipment, so that by the time they are well known, they have become very specialised indeed. These are the buyers of 300mm f/2.8 lenses, and the people who scour the top second-hand dealers for the old 1000mm f/6.3 Reflex Nikkors in order to get the extra stop-and-a-bit over the current f/11 version, even at the expense of an unmanageably small depth of field. They plant motor-driven remote-control cameras under the jumps at a horse race, or on the roof over the ring at a boxing match.

Ideally, you should participate (or have participated) in the sports you photograph; at the very least, you should spend a long time watching and learning before you try any serious photography. Knowledge of the game enables you to anticipate the action, which is critical when even the 1/30 second between pressing the shutter release and actually taking the picture can be the difference between a great picture and an also-ran. It also helps you to avoid the one unforgivable crime among sports photographers, namely getting in the way of the players or distracting them. At the very least this is discourteous, stupid, and counter-productive (because you are unlikely to be allowed to photograph there again), and at worst it can be fatal: one photographer was killed when he blinded an oncoming rally-driver at night with his flashgun.

Sports stock photography for general libraries is only rarely concerned with the big events (though the major sports libraries do cover these, and sell news pictures to magazines and newspapers). More often, the important thing is the gesture, the movement, or the kicked-up dust that symbolises the game. The pain on the face of an athlete as he draws on his last reserves of strength is the same whether he is a world-class runner or someone from the local club; the drama of a runner sliding into home base can be the same whether he is a great star or a weekend player. Neither cricket

Famous personalities are news at the time – and valuable stock shots later, when (for example) biographies of the personalities, or histories of the sport, or even magazines and part-works, are written.

It is often possible to convey a great deal about a sport by showing the spectators, with the game going on in the background; but it is a mistake to concentrate only on pictures of the spectators, as demand for action shots is often higher.

With the increase in the popularity of ballooning, balloon photographs are now much easier to obtain than they used to be, and standards have risen. The only way to get a picture like this is from another balloon: aerostatists never take off near high buildings if they can help it, and the havoc which a helicopter would cause does not bear thinking about.

Whenever a sport becomes fashionable, there is an immediate upsurge of demand for pictures; the only way to cash in on this is to jump on to the bandwagon as fast as possible. In this case, a waterproof Nikonos camera would have been ideal.

on the village green nor little-league baseball is likely to attract world-class sports photographers, yet both can be readily saleable subjects. By concentrating on the typical, and especially on the timeless, you can get pictures that will sell again and again.

If you look at the work of the great sports photographers, you will find four common factors: an impeccable sense of timing; simple graphic compositions without extraneous material in the picture; uncluttered backgrounds (often difficult to find, but achievable with differential focus); and the suggestion of movement by panning, controlled blur, or an impossibly frozen pose – it is all too easy to get a picture that looks as if someone is just standing there. Clip testing, rather than bracketing, is usual in action photography, as there may be only one opportunity to capture an event. Resist the temptation to overshoot unnecessarily, and edit your pictures carefully before submitting them to the picture library.

Nature

There are a few naturalist-photographers whose names are well-known outside their immediate fields: Hosking's bird photography, Dalton's frozen-motion studies, and the seemingly all-round brilliance of Heather Angel immediately spring to mind. All of them made their names as specialists, which is normally the case in nature work. Even the glamorous subjects, such as big game, tend to be the province of specialists, because in order to get the very best pictures you need to be very knowledgeable about your subject. 'Biologist first, photographer second' is a phrase you will often hear among successful nature photographers.

For the most part, it is a world of specialised and specially adapted equipment, such as the ultra-long lenses used by bird photographers, the special macro apparatus used by entomologists, the Nikonos cameras and underwater housings used by divers, and the oil-immersion objectives and vibration-free leaf-shutter adapters used by microscopists. It is not a world open to the casual photographer whose real interests lie elsewhere, except for the rare lucky shot in the case of some of the larger, easier and more photogenic animals.

If, however, you are a biologist with a collection of first-class pictures, the rewards can be good. There are several specialist libraries that may be able to handle your work more effectively than a general library, and picture researchers are also used to approaching individuals who have good collections of their own pictures. The main difficulty for many biologists lies in recognising which of their pictures are likely to be saleable, and whether it would be better to use a general library. Most libraries can help you with the first decision but the latter question is a matter of deciding for yourself.

It is usual to distinguish between 'diagnostic' pictures, which clearly show the shape, markings, colours, and other distinctive or 'diagnostic' characteristics of a particular plant or animal and are mainly of interest to other biologists, and 'dramatic' or 'mood' pictures that are more compositionally and aesthetically interesting. It used to be possible to sell the diagnostic pictures to text-books and specialist magazines, and dramatic or mood pictures to non-specialist markets, but over the last few

years there have been dramatic improvements in equipment and techniques, and consequently a massive upward revision of expectations. Nowadays diagnosis and drama are expected to be combined as a matter of course, except in the most rigorous and specialised text-books, and mood pictures have to be very good indeed. In

There are enough bird-watchers who are also highly competent photographers that bird photography is not a field for the casual amateur. Furthermore, accurate captioning is *essential*, and unless you are already a bird fantic, you may find this very tiresome.

A feeding lion is a surprisingly easy subject; once he has his teeth into the food, he will be distracted only by the most pressing matters. If you want to practice animal photography, feeding time at the zoo offers some of the best opportunities.

Although elephants are remarkably photogenic, and seem very gentle in zoos, it is worth remembering just how much damage they can do if they are alarmed in the wild. Also, if the photographer had not used a long lens, he would very probably have frightened away the birds which eat the ticks off the elephants' backs and the insects which the elephants' feeding disturbs.

Amphibians are not everyone's favourite animals, but you need a real feeling for them if you are going to photograph them successfully. The other things you need include patience and a good tolerance of getting wet!

Insect photography, with its combination of ultra-close work, fast-moving and easily-frightened subjects, and virtually zero depth of field, is one of the most technically demanding forms of natural history photography.

other words, unless your photographs are very, very good, there is probably someone else around who is better.

If you want to get involved in this sort of photography, and have no experience at all, an excellent place to start is your local zoo, especially if it is the open-plan type with moats and ditches, rather than bars, to keep you away from the animals. Go back to the same animal several times and try to learn its habits and the best way to photograph it. You will soon find out if you have the patience to get involved in real nature photography, which is much more demanding in every way.

Animals

There is also a large market for pictures of domestic animals of all kinds, as has already been mentioned in the last chapter. Here we are concerned with photographing animals out of doors and in other environments than the studio. The main markets are for dogs, cats, and horses, but two little-considered categories are farm and working animals. For all animals, there are certain basic guidelines – like people in stock shots they must look happy, healthy, and lively – but if you are photographing show animals, you must also know enough about the breed to know what to look for. The client who buys the picture may or may not know enough to spot these points, but his readers almost certainly will, and they can be very critical.

Dogs may be required on their own – running, sitting and looking alert, jumping – or with people. A man and his dog, a child and a puppy, and a beautiful woman with a pair of aristocratic dogs such as Borzois or Afghans, can find all sorts of markets, mainly for advertising or editorial use. The most difficult shot is probably the running dog. Actually getting it to run is

Early morning is often one of the best times to photograph horses; they are usually alert without being skittish, and morning light (or better still, morning mist) provides excellent backgrounds.

seldon a problem – most dogs love to fetch sticks – but the speed with which it moves, and the relatively small size of the animal, can mean that you use a great deal of film to get a single shot.

There is rather less demand for cats, which is just as well, as they are contrary creatures, and trying to get a picture of a cat stalking or jumping is far from easy. You are faced not only with the difficulty of photographing it, but also with making it do what you want. There is, however, a fair sized (if not particularly lucrative) market for cats doing the strange yet graceful things which cats sometimes do, such as shadow-boxing with themselves in a mirror or jumping after a fluffy toy mouse, held on a piece of string just above their reach. Stock pictures can be fun, but often pictures like these are taken for purely commmercial reasons.

Photographs of horses (other than working horses) fall into two categories: sport/action and general. Action pictures of horse racing are very much like action pictures in any sport, though the techniques are an odd amalgam of those required for motor sport and those required for human athletic events. General pictures are often more saleable; horses in a meadow make a classically tranquil scene, which can be used for many purposes. Advertising campaigns often centre on an unrestrained getaway image and horses are wonderful subjects for these clients.

Farm animals are surprisingly difficult to photograph, largely because of the extraordinary ugliness of the average modern farm; rustic wood has given way to corrugated iron, concrete, and steel fencing. If you have the good fortune to find an old-fashioned farm, you can get attractive pastoral scenes (which are the ones that sell). Otherwise, even if you can persuade the farmer to let you place his animals in more attractive surroundings, you may have some difficulty in persuading your subjects to go where you want them. Cows are amenable enough, under the guidance of a good herdsman, but pigs are inclined to be self-willed, and in a

The amiable and intelligent pig, decked with flowers and a model mother; the quiet and thoughtful cow. Pictures like these can easily distract us from the unpleasant truth, which is that we keep both for food. Before taking pictures of farm animals, you have to think carefully about what you are trying to say.

confrontation a quarter of a ton of sow has the upper trotter. Working animals, such as sheepdogs and brewers' dray horses (which can look very picturesque indeed) are normally so well trained that it is only a question of explaining to the owner what you want.

Finally, pictures of animals with the vet sell surprisingly well, provided there is nothing too obviously wrong with them: the anxious queue of owners waiting outside, and the vet examining the animals, are the prime shots.

Historical

Historical pictures fall into several categories. Some are genuinely old pictures of people, events, and places as they were in the more or less distant past. Assembling a library of pictures like this is more a matter of collecting than of photography, and unless you have in mind a special topic – royalty, militaria, or Victorian pornography, for example – you are unlikely to be able to compete with such major established collections as the Radio Times Hulton Picture Library, Keystone Photos, or the various university collections in the United States. With the more recent pictures, you must also be careful about copyright.

You can however build up a useful library of 'instant history', by concentrating on those aspects of society that are changing or disappearing. Even the most commonplace subjects will become intriguing if they are kept for long enough; think back to a shop interior of your youth, or a street scene with the cars of only 30 years ago. When an old building is demolished to make way for the new; when you find an artisan following some craft that has all but vanished, like thatching or general black-smithing and farriery; when a whole area is affected by a road-building scheme; when a new factory or dock is opened, or a ship launched; these are the times when you can photograph history in the making.

As noted at the beginning of this chapter, the library use of these pictures is usually secondary. Normally, they will already have been used in an original article or book, and then put in the library to earn additional income. Rewards may also be slow in coming, for obvious reasons, but unlike most library collections, where

pictures become dated and less saleable, this sort of photograph actually improves with keeping.

A third variety of historical photograph is a modern picture of something old. There are many possibilities here, but one of the most obvious is vintage motor cars, for which there is quite a large, but not very well paying, market. Good pictures of old cars, with uncluttered backgrounds, no anachronisms, and accurate captions, are frequently requested. When you look at some of the illustrations in books, it is not hard to see why: the most common fault is a horizon that neatly follows the line of the top of the car, bisecting the picture and visually separating the driver's head from his shoulders. A slightly lower viewpoint would give a background of sky; a slightly higher one, a background of road or grass. Either would be preferable to the eye-level disasters so often seen. Of course, this also applies to many other subjects: insufficient attention to the background and surroundings (road signs, litter, etc.) can ruin any picture.

Pictures of old cars (and motorcycles, traction engines and canal boats) cannot, however, be taken at most public rallies. The cars are too close together, and there are unsightly placards and rope fences to keep people from getting too close to the vehicles, but do not keep them out of the picture, the owners are rarely posed or dressed in a way that will add to the picture rather than detract from it. You can take some general pictures at rallies, usually either long shots or medium close-ups, but for pictures of the cars in classic surroundings, it is best to

Mount Rushmore is a fascinating monument; and how much more fascinating would it be to see the sculptors working on their massive masks? If there is any major project under way near you, it is an excellent idea to document it as far as possible, for future years.

Spinning and weaving enjoy considerable status as creative crafts; the caption should make it clear who the craftsman or craftswoman is, and where the picture was taken.

Thatching and coopering are both crafts which are far less important than they used to be, yet they continue to survive. They may yet stage a comeback – but until they do, they remain to show us how the past lingers into the present, and time is a continuous stream.

Fotobank International has a small but useful specialist collection of photographs of vintage motorcycles. The nucleus was no more than a few dozen photographs, originally taken to illustrate a book, which were placed *en bloc* in the library after they had been used for their original purpose.

Indians of a different kind. Many Native American villages recreate the lifestyle which their forbears followed a hundred years ago; an Indian special collection might include pictures like this, photographs of traditional artefacts and clothes, and pictures of the more modern side of Indian life, such as education and agriculture.

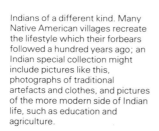

contact the owner (a photocopied circular letter is useful) and arrange a specific shooting session. Most people are delighted to help; they like to show off their pride and joy and they know that if it appears in a book or magazine article, it will enhance its value. Make negatives from the three or four best shots and send the prints as a thank-you.

Even if you do not already have a specific field of interest, there is scope in this sort of photography for building up a good collection of specialist pictures. A moment's thought will provide a dozen possibilities: prehistoric settlements and stone circles, stained glass, old bar interiors, ancient buildings, farm vehicles, antique costumes, pewterware, Art Deco, time-pieces, vintage cameras, or sundials. You will do best if you try to build up a good number of pictures of a few subjects, rather than spreading yourself too thinly. This is a simple matter of marketing; as already emphasised, picture researchers and other buyers tend to go for the sources they know for particular subjects, and if you can make your library the place for canals and canal boats, you can possibly upstage other libraries which only offer a few pictures of the same subjects. However, do not underestimate the difficulty of handling your own administration. Check with other photographers who have tried it.

There is also a small market for pictures that re-create the past – not fakes, but photographs that capture the mood and atmosphere of bygone times. Staging such pictures, as advertising agencies sometimes do, can be immensely expensive if you have to hire everything; but if you know of somewhere that could, with a little effort, be made to look authentic, or if you have access to a collection of antique clothing or vintage bicycles, you may be able to cash in comparatively cheaply on the popularity of nostalgia. The past does not need to be very distant – a few greasy friends with an assortment of Tritons, Bonnies and Goldies can recreate the Ace Cafe motorcycling scene of the early 1960s. Most people like dressing up, and getting such a picture together could be fun – many motorcycle clubs would join in just for the sake of a picture. On its own, such a picture (or rather, set of pictures) might not be much use, but it could form a useful basis for an article. Combine it with static shots of a few vintage and classic machines, and perhaps some genuinely old pictures from the early days of motorcycling, and you have the nucleus of a promising special collection. Record covers are often made up from this type of 're-created' picture.

In more and more places, old customs are being revived; in some places they are actual re-creations of the past, and in others they are re-interpretations of an old idea. Taken together with those customs which never have died out, such events could form the basis of a special collection.

Art and Artefacts

Art, in the usual sense of the word – paintings, etchings, sculpture and the like – is rarely a profitable field for the stock photographer. All of the more important pictures and sculptures tend to be either in public collections, where there will be an official photographer on the payroll or an 'understanding' with a professional nearby, or in private collections where they are totally inaccessible. Of course, it is worth trying to become the person with whom they have their understanding, but this is another matter. Libraries which do specialise in this field usually shoot their own pictures or have a 'staff' photographer.

There is, however, a fair market in many less obvious fields. For example, any kind of ethnic, primitive, or folk art may find a ready sale, both for editorial use and for such publications as travel brochures. The important thing to worry about here is copyright, for obvious reasons.

Lighting *objects d'art*, especially paintings, is more difficult than it might seem, largely because of the danger of flashback (reflections from the glossy surface of the paint, enamel, or textured porcelain). Polarised light sources, and a polariser on the camera, are the approved route. An easier and more profitable field to explore may be the photography of other antiquities and applied arts: arms and armour, fine bindings on old books, religious ikons and statues, old wood-cuts, and so forth – anything which you would expect to find in a museum, art gallery or historical library.

Admittedly, museums and galleries do have their own photographic sections, but library pictures are far more attractive on the grounds of speed, lack of paperwork, and often quality. The usual procedure in a museum (with a few honourable exceptions) is that you find the object you want in the museum, identify it by its accession number, fill in a request (often in duplicate or triplicate), and then wait an indeterminate number of weeks for a photograph that may be exactly what you want – or may be completely useless. About the only advantages of the official institutions are the sheer range of choice,

Statues such as this one, which lend themselves to humorous or bawdy interpretations (or to Women's Lib polemics), can actually be easier to sell than more serious works. This picture also illustrates a common difficulty with photographing immovable works of art, namely lighting which is less than ideal from a photographic point of view. Fill-in flash, or at least a reflector, plus a polarising filter to control reflections, might have been worth considering.

and the usually modest prices, but they have no idea of deadlines at all. Any enterprising photographer who borrows goods from a friendly local antique dealer, private collector, or commercial art gallery is well ahead of the game in the picture researcher's book.

If you do enter this field, do not neglect humbler artefacts such as knives, children's games and toys (especially dolls), or kitchen impedimenta, and be alive to the possibility of constructing still-life pictures, or even sets with people, such as a little girl playing with the dolls. The techniques for this are similar to those required for other studio shots, as covered in the previous chapter, though the marketing is necessarily different; once again, you have to get yourself known (or put your pictures into a library that is known) as the provider of such pictures, and this may not be easy, given the wide-ranging but numerically limited market.

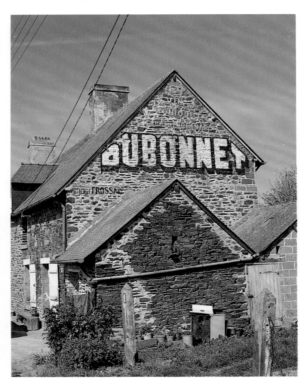

Details, particularly of frescos and the like, are often much easier to "read" than a picture of the whole thing, though small or miniature paintings obviously work well in their entirety, complete with frame. Paradoxically, the best-selling picture here is likely to be the advertisement for Dubonnet, which scarcely even aspires to being folk art, but which does sum up a great deal about rural France.

Black and White

With the ever-increasing use of colour, black and white is becoming a more and more specialist requirement in the world of stock photography. This is why it is covered in this chapter, even though it is a medium rather than a subject. It invariably costs more to produce than colour, yet often earns less; black and white rates are traditionally between a half and two-thirds of colour rates, though it is increasingly common for libraries to make no distinction at all.

Nevertheless, there is still plenty of demand for monochrome stock pictures, most of it from book publishers and specialist periodicals, though there is also quite a good market in company reports. Astonishingly, most photographic magazines still use more black and white than colour, and magazines devoted to other hobbies and interests may use little or no colour other than on the cover. Similarly, the demand for black and white pictures in most books still outweighs the demand for colour, except in the 'coffee table' market.

Most stock photographers will normally work exclusively in colour, and simply make a black and white conversion from a transparency when it is needed. Or, better still, they will let the buyer do it. For this, a medium-format original is all but essential: the quality loss during conversion will be very evident if the original was on 35mm. Otherwise, for most applications, medium-speed black and white 35mm film is more than adequate.

Pictures for reproduction should not be 'bright' or 'plucky' or any of the other euphemisms for 'too contrasty'. Excessive contrast may be necessary for low-quality newspaper reproduction, but for any other application the print should contain a full range of tones, or even be slightly soft in contrast. It is easy to increase contrast in the printing process, but virtually impossible to lose excessive contrast. Glossy paper, preferably glazed, is best, and the standard sizes are 10 x 8″ or the old 8½ x 6½″ 'whole plate'. Anything larger is hard to

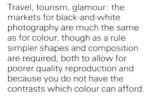

Travel, tourism, glamour: the markets for black-and-white photography are much the same as for colour, though as a rule simpler shapes and composition are required, both to allow for poorer quality reproduction and because you do not have the contrasts which colour can afford.

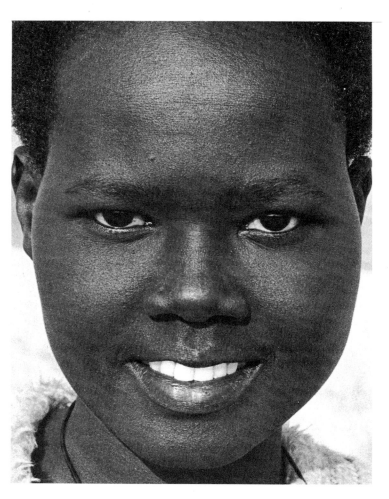

Faces are always useful fillers, and this close-up study of a young black boy could be used for many kinds of editorial purposes. The picture on the Chelsea Embankment (below) is rather more specific, but it could be used to create a mood as well as to illustrate an article on London, sculpture, or dramatic composition.

handle, and should not be submitted unless specially requested; anything smaller is fiddly and does not allow maximum reproduction quality. Leave a small border of up to ¼″ (6mm) for handling, and stick the caption to the back of the print; writing directly on the back, especially with a ball-point pen, is almost certain to show through on the other side. Rather than use a rubber stamp, which may mark the face of the print behind, use a self-adhesive label for your name and address.

Ever fewer commercial libraries still handle black and white, and those that do usually send out a fresh repro-quality black and white print to each client; prints that sell well are normally ordered in tens, and the stock replenished when it falls low. Remember, too, that many specialist magazines pay laughably low rates, and that most libraries refuse to deal with such publications because they would make a loss on each sale. Ask yourself if the game is really worth the candle.

Other Subjects

Dance, industrial photography, girls, sailing, science and technology, personalities, agriculture, food, drink, individual countries or even cities: we have only begun to touch upon the vast range of subjects which have been successfully exploited in specialist collections. This chapter could be expanded to fill another book and still not provide anything like a comprehensive coverage. What we have done instead is to provide a number of useful examples, and to show how pictorial standards are not relaxed merely because you are selling to specialist markets.

No doubt, you have your own ideas on subjects. For example, a pilot might well consider aerial photography (but possibly only as a passenger), while a farmer would be well placed to deal with agricultural subjects. Many people will find that they can 'cash in' on interests and hobbies, and professionals can often take pictures for stock while they are working on commissioned shoots of a specialised nature. Amateurs may be able to take pictures in the course of their everyday work: someone em-

ployed in a foundry, for example, could get some excellent and well-informed industrial pictures.

It is important to realise that you will have to work hard if you want to get good pictures; merely taking them in passing is unlikely to be enough. If this begins to interfere with your other work, then your employer may quite properly complain, though there is a way to take pictures on the firm's time, with the firm's approval. Most large companies run house magazines or newspapers, and the editors are always desperate for good pictures (and good copy too, for that matter). You can shoot your own stock material while taking black-and-whites for the house journal. Amateurs can, however, run into difficulties if the company then wants to use their pictures for publicity or advertising. First, the pictures must be as good as (or better than) the ones that they normally use, and secondly, there is the question of a fair rate for the job. There is the ethical matter of stealing work from established professionals (though professionals show no compunction in stealing work themselves, and only squeal when they are the losers), and the purely practical point that once low rates or free pictures are established, the company is not going to be willing to pay anyone a reasonable rate. On the other hand, it seems churlish to refuse permission to use your pictures when they have helped you to get them. The best thing is to make it clear at the outset that the pictures for the house journal are free (as they invariably have to be), and that any advertising or promotional use will have to be handled by your library, though perhaps at preferential rates.

There is one golden rule, however: concentrate on the general and the timeless rather than on the particular and the topical. There are news stock agencies, it is true, and news photographs may in time become stock photographs, and earn more in the long run than they did when first published, but for the most part it is easier to sell a picture that is clear, simple, and easily understood (both visually and intellectually) than one that is actually more informative, but hard to read. Although this is a general rule, it is one that is well worth repeating here; if you want to know why, just look through a few special-interest books and magazines.

Popcorn, anyone? Portfolio shots can be stock shots too, and although this picture took a good deal of time to realise, it is not hard to imagine a number of possible uses.

170

Ultra-modern combine harvesters devour acres of land; but how long will they last? Will we see fully-automated farming, as some say, or a return to the land and to traditional ways, as others predict? Or, more likely, will both come to replace these overgrown automobiles? The present is forever becoming the past.

Agriculture and farming could be the basis for a massive special collection, whether with reportage-type shots like this or moody, impressionistic landscapes. You should never pick a subject merely because it has commercial appeal, however; unless you actually have an interest yourself, you are unlikely to be as successful as someone who does care.

Although most men have more than a passing interest in pretty girls and attractive women, they are another subject to be avoided unless you are sure that you can do justice to them. Many of the best photographers of women are women; photographing their own sex gives them a different perspective from men, and one which is often commercially successful.

Chapter 10

PREPARING A SUBMISSION

There is a great difference, both psychologically and practically, between preparing the initial submission to a library and preparing subsequent submissions. The initial submission is, after all, what the library judges the photographer on; with subsequent submissions, there is some sort of working relationship and the parties know each other and what to expect.

At the very beginning a chicken-and-egg relationship exists between selecting the pictures and submitting them to the library. Unless the photographer has the material to submit, there is little point in approaching a library; until he approaches a library, he may not have any very clear idea about what to submit.

It should be fairly clear from the previous chapters of this book what is likely to sell, and what is not. But to get down to specifics: which of your pictures should you select and how should you submit them? To begin with, it is essential to have enough material. This is a very flexible term, but it means being able to submit at least 50 pictures, and preferably more, for the first submission. If your pictures are unbelievably good, the library may be prepared to take as few as a dozen or two; at the other extreme, some libraries insist on a minimum submission of 200 or even 500 pictures, in order to discourage people who imagine that they can raid their old files for all their best snaps, put them together and send them in to a picture library. Most picture editors agree that such libraries do themselves a disservice, in that it should be perfectly possible to tell from 50 or 100 pictures what sort of photographer they are dealing with. The concept of 'enough' material does, however, embrace the need to have a clear theme or themes in the submission: unless he can see clear evidence of this, the picture editor may quite reasonably assume that the photographer *has* merely raided all his old files.

In an initial submission of 100 pictures, there might be only one theme, or there might be as many as 10 or 12. The important thing would be to group all related pictures together, so that the picture editor could see how a particular subject was treated – the depth that the photographer went into, the use of differing viewpoints, ideas, and compositional shapes, and (equally important) what has been omitted. The ideal number of themes would probably be four

or five, enough to show the photographer's versatility without running the risk of appearing superficial. It would also be a good idea to put in a few 'one-offs', pictures that were not related to any particular theme. Ten or a dozen such pictures could show how the photographer approached different subjects, and might also provide a departure point for suggestions from the picture techniques, ideas, or approaches which might usefully be pursued.

In most cases, the best approach is to write to the picture library of your choice, and ask if you might come along and talk to one of their picture editors. Ask if you should bring any pictures; explain that you think it might be a better idea not to bring any along at first, as you want to explore their requirements before you make your selection. There may be an exchange of letters or telephone calls before your visit, but you will almost invariably be made welcome. As we have repeatedly stressed, the picture library needs photographers just as much as the photographer needs a picture library.

At the preliminary meeting, treat the whole proceedings as two job interviews. On the one hand, the library is interviewing you to find out if they can use your work, on the other, you are interviewing them to find out if they can sell it for you. Ask to see pictures from their files on topics related to your own. This will not only show you the kind and standard of work which they handle, but it can also save you the embarrassment of submitting similar or inferior pictures. If they do ask you to bring pictures along, do not bring too many, and be sure to have them carefully organised.

After this meeting, you should be in a position to make your selection for them. The criteria for selection should already be clear from what has already been said in this book, but a few guidelines are worth repeating – they will be especially valuable in later submissions, where you will probably be selecting from a smaller number of pictures, perhaps the product of a single shoot. First, weed out any in which the exposure does not achieve the desired effect; note that we do not say 'wrong' exposures, because sometimes exposures that are technically 'wrong' can be aesthetically right. Remember, too, that slides that are ⅓-½ stop underexposed are often the ones which reproduce best: if in

doubt, go for the 'heavier' transparency. Secondly, weed out all the pictures with other technical defects, paying special attention to camera shake. Thirdly, remove slides that are obviously badly composed, or that have obtrusive extraneous material in the picture. Finally, make value judgements about similar pictures: it may be all right to submit two or three with only slight variations, and it is actually a good idea to submit similar pictures in vertical and horizontal formats, but presenting the picture editor with a dozen similar pictures of the same thing will not endear you to him.

Once you have sorted out your pictures, the next question is how to mount them. Opinions vary, but probably the neatest, easiest, quickest and cheapest way is to use multi-pocket sleeves. The standard sizes hold 20-35mm mounted (or unmounted) slides, or 12 rollfilm transparencies, or four 4 x 5″ transparencies. A useful tip is to use only half of the pockets, with the other

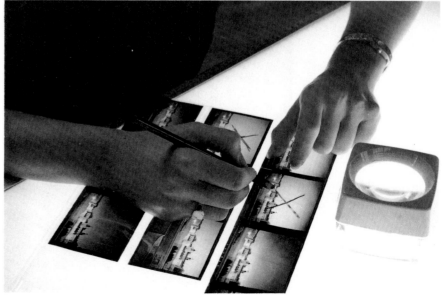

half containing the captions, for 120 and 4x5″ slides. With 35mm, it is usually as well to write the caption on the slide mount, and to stamp your name and the international copyright symbol (©) on it as well.

Of the other options, there is no doubt that the individual black or coloured masks, held in acetate sleeves, are the most impressive. Some libraries are more than happy to accept these, while others refuse to use them and strip the pictures out so that they can mount them in their own sleeves. As these masks are expensive, check the library's policy before using them. Another possibility, which some libraries may prefer, is for you to present your pictures in their own style of mount. This is normally only possible once you have a working relationship with the library. Otherwise, they are likely to be unwilling to give away their mounts.

Many photographers prefer to take their submission along to the library themselves, and if you live close to the library, or at least visit the area reasonably often, this may be the best idea, but do telephone to arrange an appointment first. Otherwise, a brief covering letter listing the number of transparencies sent should be packed in a *well-padded* envelope (any of the proprietary brands will do, preferably with some cardboard stiffening inside to give additional protection), and the whole package should be sent by some sort of insured post or carrier. British photographers have the advantage of 'consequential loss' insurance through the British Post Office, which allows claims for loss of profits, etc., should the package be lost or its contents damaged. Use FRAGILE stickers, and ones that say PHOTOGRAPHS – PLEASE DO NOT BEND; they may not be much good, but they are unlikely to do any harm. If you are sending pictures out of the country, mark them 'EXPOSED PHOTOGRAPHIC FILM – NO COMMERCIAL VALUE'. This is perfectly true from the Customs point of view, as they levy duty only on the intrinsic value (the cost of the film) and not the extrinsic value, the value of the images on the film.

You can now sit back and wait. Any of a number of things may happen (apart from the pictures being lost in the post). The library may decide to keep the lot, though this is unlikely. They may decide to return the lot, with or without explanation, but most probably, if the pictures are any good, they will keep some, and send back the rest with a receipt for the ones that they have kept. Some libraries will also send a guide to shooting the type of pictures they require, but they may only do this on acceptance of the pictures.

Libraries' policies on discussing rejections vary – not just according to the library, but also according to their opinion of the photographer. If they like your pictures, and want more, but think that there are certain things that you could do which would improve the saleability of your pictures, they may be prepared to discuss matters at some length. As a rule, though, it is better to wait until you know them better before pushing them for information on this point. Instead, look closely at the rejected pictures as soon as they arrive, and try to work out why they were rejected. Could it simply be that they have other, better material, or is there some obvious fault in your photographs? Only when you have puzzled over the matter yourself for a while is it worth approaching them.

When your first submission has been accepted, at least in part, all you have to do is wait for the money to roll in. However, you may have to wait a long time. To begin with, it can take several months for sales to start, and even after a sale has been made, there is the question of getting the money from the client, clearing his cheque, and paying the photographer. From the photographer's point of view, there is no doubt that libraries which provide monthly statements and cheques tend to be more attractive financially than those who work on a quarterly or half-yearly basis, but you still have to resign yourself to the fact that it may be some time before you actually see any money. And meanwhile, the library is going to want to see your next submission.

Although various points, such as presentation and subject matter, will now be clearer in the photographer's mind, the danger to guard against on the second submission is over-confidence. Because the library accepted so many of your first set of pictures, the temptation is to relax your standards a little, and send in some borderline pictures which you would have rejected in the first submission. Furthermore, because you are selecting from a smaller pool of pictures, and because the memory of shooting them is clearer in your mind, there is a natural

tendency to over-value doubtful ones. As you get to know the library better, you may be able to get away with this: at first, however, it can seriously damage your credibility.

A good guideline for the size of second and subsequent submissions is to send between 50 and 100 pictures in a batch. There are two reasons for this. One is that anyone's critical faculties are dulled by having to go through too many pictures, and this applies equally to you and to the picture editor at the library. The other is that by keeping your submissions small, and by carefully going through what was rejected, you can build up a clearer idea of what is wanted and what is not. If you build up a really good relationship with the picture editor, he may even go through a submission with you, explaining why he rejects some and takes others, though this will depend very much on the personalities involved.

Remember, though, that one man's meat is another man's poison, and do not expect always to agree with or even to understand the picture editor's judgements. There are as many points of view as there are photographers, picture editors, and clients; and at the end of the day your success will be measured in hard cash, which by definition is what any form of professional photography is all about.

APPENDICES

Appendix 1

The BIPP model release form is a typical example, widely used by British photographers; similar forms are recommended by professional bodies throughout the world, and in some countries, pre-printed pads are available. The BIPP version is unusually comprehensive, and very considerate of the needs of the model, which is why it is reproduced here by kind permission of the Institute. Further enquiries about the BIPP should be directed to:

The General Secretary,
British Institute of Professional Photography,
Amwell End, Ware, Hertfordshire, SG12 9HN.
Telephone Ware (0920) 4011

Notes on the BIPP Release

1 If the photographer is working with an assistant, and the assistant takes any photographs on his own account, it may be advisable to complete another model release, but if the pictures are taken solely as an assistant, one form is enough.

2 This section, and the next, are to ensure that the pictures are not used for any other purpose than that agreed, though it is of course possible to enter the name of the photographer here and "STOCK" in the next section.

3 This is, in its nature, a limited release: this section would need to be deleted in order to make it a general release – or write STOCK in here.

4, 5 These are simply useful control information for the photographer, though they could also be useful in determining exactly which pictures were taken for what purpose, in the event of a dispute.

6 It is particularly important to fill this in if you repeatedly work with the same model, for obvious reasons.

7 This sum may be nominal, or it may be enormous; note the provision for "any other sums which may become due"; these should be clearly agreed beforehand.

8 Another set of limitations on use: the best thing to do for stock photography would be to tick all (or rather, delete none), or to add ANY USE – STOCK PHOTOGRAPHY under *Worldwide.

9 This is self explanatory; it is only very rarely that you would want to use the model's name, but it might be the case if (for example) you wanted her to endorse a product.

10 Very useful with amateur models, who sometimes think they do!

11 The age of contractual majority varies from place to place; check local law on this one.

12 This section is self-explanatory; the witness is not invariably legally required, but will make life much easier in the event of a dispute.

British Institute of Professional Photography

British Institute of
Professional Photography
Amwell End
Ware, Hertfordshire
SG12 9HN

Tel: Ware 0920 4011

SPECIMEN ONLY

Standard Release Form For Signature By Models

Founded in 1901

1 Name of photographer

2 Name of *Advertising agency/client

3 Product, Service or Purpose

4 Negative Series No.   Order No. **5**   Date **6**

In consideration the sum of £ **7** and any other sums which may become due to me under the British Institute of Professional Photography current Terms, Conditions and Standards for the engagement of professional models in still photography, and conditionally upon due payment of the aforesaid sums and the undertaking of the Advertising Agency/ Client/ Photographer given below,

I permit the Advertising Agency/Client/ Photographer and its licensees or assignees to use the photograph(s) referred to above and/or drawings therefrom and any other reproductions or adaptations thereof either complete or in part, alone or in conjunction with any wording and/or drawings solely and exclusively for:

8 * **Editorial**

   * **Experimental**

   * **PR**

   * **Press Advertising**

   * **Poster Advertising (4 sheet upwards)**

   * **Display Material and Posters (under 4 sheet)** in relation to the above product, service or purpose

   * **In the United Kingdom**

   * **In Europe**

   * **Worldwide**

* Model must delete if not applicable.

----

9 I understand that such copyright material shall be deemed to represent an imaginary person unless agreed, in writing, by my agent or myself.

10 I understand that I do not own the copyright of the photograph(s)   **11** * I am over 18 years of age.

Name (in Capitals)

Signature of model

12 Address / Agent

Date   Witness

Models who are under 18 years of age must produce evidence of consent by their parent or guardian.

In accepting the above release * Advertising Agency/ Client/Photographer undertakes that the copyright material shall only be used in accordance with the terms of the release.

Delivery Note

The delivery note shown here is the old Foto-bank pre-computer version, which is made up as a three-piece carbonless set. It is self explanatory, and the terms and conditions are printed on the back, as shown.

The Terms and Conditions are based on BAPLA (British Association of Picture Libraries and Agencies) recommendations; all reputable British libraries use a similar form.

A separate sheet, detailing the holding fees, service charges, and other financial conditions is enclosed with the order; this is supplementary to the Terms and Conditions, and is to be signed and returned by the client both as acknowledgement of receipt and as acceptance of Fotobank's terms and conditions. Obviously, the fees are updated from time to time – this is a fairly old specimen!

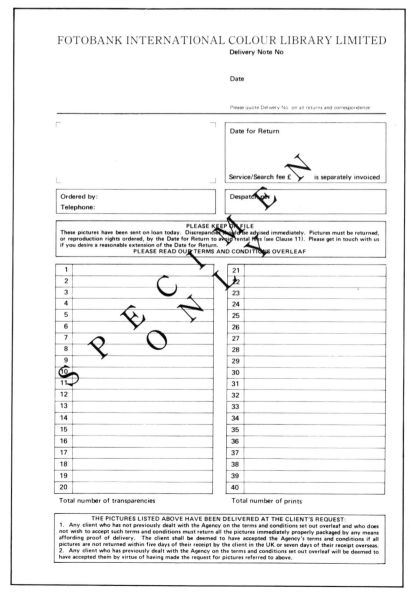

TERMS AND CONDITIONS OF SUBMISSION AND REPRODUCTION OF PICTURES

1. In this Agreement the terms (a) **picture** includes a photograph, transparency, negative, design, artwork, painting, montage, drawing, engraving, or any other item which the Agency may offer for the purpose of reproduction; (b) **reproduction** includes any form of publication or copying of the whole or part of any picture whether by printing, photography, slide projection (whether or not to an audience), xerography, artist's reference, artist's illustration, layout or presentation, electronic or mechanical reproduction or by any other means; (c) **Date for Return** is the date by which the pictures supplied by the Agency must be returned to it as specified on the advice or delivery note or invoice or as extended by notice in writing from the Agency. If no date is specified, the Date for Return shall be four weeks from the date of the delivery note or if an invoice is rendered for reproduction rights 12 weeks from the date of such invoice; (d) the **agency** is the supplier of the pictures.

2. No variation of any term or condition set out herein shall be effective unless agreed in writing by both parties. The Agency's catalogue, prospectus or other advertising material does not form part of this Agreement.

3. Pictures are supplied on **loan** and no property or copyright in any picture shall pass to the Client whether on its submission or on the Agency's grant of reproduction rights in respect thereof.

4. A non-refundable **service fee** to cover administrative costs and dispatch of the pictures is payable by the Client on each submission and re-submission of pictures whether or not reproduction rights are required or granted. An additional fee may be charged to cover research time spent by the Agency (see Note 1 below). The Client shall pay for courier, express or any other special delivery arrangement requested.

5. **Reproduction rights** (if and when granted) are strictly limited to the use, period of time and territory specified on the Agency's invoice and unless otherwise agreed in writing relate to a single publication in a single size with text (if any) in one language only. Rights granted to reproduce a picture on a product do not include the right to use that picture directly or indirectly in any manner in the advertising of that product unless such right is specifically granted.

6. Reproduction rights granted are **personal** to the Client and may not be assigned, nor may any picture submitted to the Client be loaned or transferred to third parties save for the purpose of the exercise by the Client of such reproduction rights.

7. The Agency's **advice or delivery** note will list all the pictures delivered to the Client, which shall be presumed to have been received in good condition, unless within 2 days of receipt the Client notifies the Agency in writing of any discrepancy or damage.

8. (a) Risk in and responsibility for pictures passes to the Client from the time they are received. The Client shall immediately inform the Agency in writing of any known **loss** or **misuse** of, or **damage** to the pictures while in the Client's possession or that of any third party. If a picture is not returned within 12 weeks of the Date for Return then the Agency may in its sole discretion presume it to be lost (see Note 2 below).

(b) The Client shall be liable to pay the Agency **compensation** in respect of each picture lost or damaged. Such compensation shall be £400 for each picture lost or damaged with the exception of any monotone picture for which there is an available negative in which case the compensation shall be £25 and with the further exception of any picture in respect of which a different compensation figure for loss or serious damage has previously been specified in writing by the Agency. Payment of compensation does not give rise to any rights in any picture.

(c) A picture subsequently **found** must be returned to the Agency immediately. If it is undamaged the Client will be credited with the compensation paid less a rental fee (under Clause 11) from the date the compensation is claimed to the date the picture is returned, such credit being at least 20% of the compensation paid.

9. Any picture returned without its mount or with its caption or other mount data missing or defaced shall incur a **replacement charge** of £15.

10. The Client must return every picture to the Agency by its **Date for Return** by any method affording proof of delivery. All necessary protection must be given to pictures in transit. A delivery note listing and totalling the returned pictures must be enclosed, and an advice in writing with this same information sent by separate post.

11. Unless otherwise agreed each picture may be held by the Client rental free until its Date for Return and thereafter the Client shall be liable to pay a **rental fee** of £3.50 per picture per week or part thereof pending its return (see Note 3 below). Payment of the rental fee does not entitle the Client to retain the picture after the Date for Return.

12. (a) Until the Agency has invoiced the reproduction fee neither party is committed to grant or to acquire any reproduction rights in any picture. After a fee has been agreed and an invoice issued there is a firm and binding contract whereby the Agency is committed to grant **reproduction rights** and the Client to acquire them. If after such invoicing but before payment, the Client requests **cancellation** of the reproduction rights the Agency may in its discretion cancel subject to the Client paying a cancellation fee (see Note 4 below).

(b) The Client's **right to reproduce** a picture arises only when the Agency's invoice relating to the grant of such right is fully paid. Any reproduction before payment of the invoice constitutes an infringement of rights and a breach of this Agreement entitling the Agency to rescind the Agreement and rendering the Client liable for the payment of damages (see Note 5 below).

(c) The Client agrees to **indemnify** the Agency in respect of any claims or damages or any loss or costs arising in any manner from the reproduction without proper reproduction rights of any picture supplied to the Client by the Agency.

13. If the Agency's invoice is not paid in full within 30 days of issue, the Agency may rescind this Agreement and recover damages or may charge interest on the **overdue payment** at 2½% per month. In either event the Client on request pay all costs and charges reasonably incurred in recovering any damages or overdue sum.

14. On the Client's **death or bankruptcy** or (if the Client is a company) in the event of a Resolution, Petition or Order for winding-up being made against it, or if a Receiver is appointed, the Agency may at any time thereafter inspect any records, accounts and books relating to the reproduction of the Agency's pictures to ensure that the pictures are being used only in accordance with the reproduction rights granted to the Client.

15. (a) Unless otherwise agreed in writing, if any picture reproduced by the Client omits the **copyright notice or credit line** specified by the Agency the reproduction fee payable by the Client shall be 20% more than that specified on the invoice.

(b) **Two proofs** of any publication or the relevant pages thereof containing any pictures supplied by the Agency are to be furnished to the Agency by the Client free of charge within 2 weeks of publication.

16. While the Agency takes all reasonable care in the performance of this Agreement generally, the Agency shall not be liable for any loss or damage suffered by the Client or by any third party arising from any defect in any picture or its caption or in any way from its reproduction.

17. Unless specified in writing no warranty is given by the Agency as to the existence or validity of model or other releases in respect of any picture and the Agency shall not be liable for the absence of such a release or for any defect in any existing releases. The Agency gives no rights or warranties with regard to the use of names, trade marks, registered or copyright designs or works of art depicted in any picture and the Client must satisfy himself that all the necessary rights or consents as may be required for reproduction are obtained. The Client shall indemnify the Agency against any loss suffered by the Agency from any reproduction of the picture by the Client without effective releases, rights or consents.

18. Reproduction rights are not granted exclusively to the Client except when specified on the invoice.

19. This **Agreement** shall be subject to and construed according to English law and the parties agree to accept the exclusive jurisdiction of the Courts of England.

NOTES

The agency is a member of the British Association of Picture Libraries and Agencies (BAPLA). These notes are BAPLA's recommendations to its members intended only for the guidance of clients and do not form part of the Terms and Conditions of the Contract.

1. BAPLA urges its members to inform the client of the amount of any service or research fee prior to the submission of pictures.

2. BAPLA urges its members to notify clients before presuming loss.

3. BAPLA urges its members to notify clients of any rental fees which are or will be payable, and thereafter to charge only in respect of those pictures not returned within 7 days of such notice.

4. BAPLA urges its members to consider favourably requests for cancellation if made within 30 days of invoice and not to charge cancellation fees exceeding 50% of the reproduction fee.

5. Damages for infringement of rights might in some cases constitute conversion damages and would ordinarily substantially exceed the appropriate reproduction fee, or provide cause for an injunction against publication.

179

ENGLAND SCENE COLOUR PICTURE LIBRARY: SPECIMEN

PLEASE READ OUR CONDITIONS OF SUBMISSION AND REPRODUCTION.

1. These transparencies are submitted on approval only.

2. Before we can agree on a fee and invoice you for reproduction rights which may be available in any of the photographs listed overleaf, you must give us details of the intended use, media, distribution area, the number of times the photograph will be published and over what period, and in the case of advertising use, the name of the advertiser must be given as well. Note that a fee must be agreed for layout and/or presentation purposes.

3. We look forward to the return within 10 days of those transparencies which are not short-listed. Unless otherwise agreed all other transparencies with the exception of those in which you have decided to purchase reproduction rights are to be returned within 28 days of receipt, failing which we retain the right to charge the following holding fees:—For the first 28 days thereafter or part thereof, £__ per transparency. For each successive 28 days thereafter or part thereof, £__ per transparency.

4. A service fee will be charged for each submission of transparencies. The precise service fee will be calculated in each case in accordance with England Scene's administrative costs and charges but will be subject to a minimum of £__.

5. Upon receipt by you of these transparencies they are held at your risk against loss, theft or damage until received back in the library which must be by registered post or by hand and suitably packed. The client shall include an advice note giving England Scene the number and/or listing of the transparencies returned therewith. You are advised to insure against loss, theft or damage.

6. Reproduction rights are offered only to you, and if purchased may not be wholly or partly sold, transferred, or disposed of to third parties without our consent.

7. Transparencies must always be returned to England Scene with their mounts whether they have been used or not. Any transparency which has been taken out of its mount or is returned without its mount or the mount data shall incur a minimum service charge of £__.

8. A charge of £__ is payable in respect of each lost, stolen or damaged transparency. In the case of a transparency which is lost but subsequently found and returned undamaged, your account will be credited with a loss fee less a holding fee of 25% thereof for each quarter or part thereof that has elapsed since the notification of such loss.

9. All reasonable care has been taken in the identification and captioning of transparencies but England Scene does not accept any liability for losses or errors of any nature whatsoever in connection therewith and it is hereby agreed that you will indemnify England Scene against any claims, loss or damages of any nature whatsoever arising out of errors in identification or captioning.

10. If any of our photographs are reproduced before we have invoiced you, a sum of £__ will be payable by way of an agreed sum for liquidated damages but such payment will not entitle you to any reproduction rights or to continued publication: nor will it entitle you to protection against claims for damage which may be made by third parties; and you shall indemnify us in respect of any claims, damages or costs arising out of any action by any other party resulting from your unauthorised publication.

11. Unless specified in writing no warranty is given by England Scene as to existence of model or other releases in respect of the transparencies. In the absence of a release being expressly stated in writing by England Scene, the client uses the transparencies at his own risk and shall indemnify England Scene against any loss occasioned by England Scene by such use.

12. England Scene makes no claim or warranty with regard to the use by the client of names or trade marks depicted in the photograph and the client must satisfy himself that all necessary permissions or consents as may be required for reproduction have been obtained.

13. No transparencies shall be copied, duplicated or reproduced in any way whatsoever nor may you part with the possession of the same in any circumstances whatsoever.

14. If any copyright licence agreement is entered into then you are to pay the agreed fee within 28 days of reproduction or within 28 days of invoice whichever is the earlier. Two copies of any reproduction shall be sent to England Scene. Transparencies in respect of which copyright licence agreement is entered into must be returned within 14 days of the first reproduction provided that under no circumstances shall such transparencies be retained by you for longer than three months after the completion of a copyright licence agreement.

15. Unless otherwise agreed a charge of 50% of the fee agreed in such copyright licence agreement will be levied on each transparency held beyond the said period of 14 days for each 6 months or part thereof during which time the transparencies are not returned.

16. In the event of your taking steps to reproduce any of the transparencies listed overleaf before payment is made against this invoice, we shall have the right to charge as agreed liquidated damages a sum equal to three times the fee for the reproduction rights, and we shall have the option to cancel reproduction rights granted.

17. In the event that payment of our invoices is not paid within 60 days of due date and that we commence litigation against you to collect the amount owing, we shall be reimbursed for reasonable legal fees.

THE ABOVE CONDITIONS ARE UNDERSTOOD TO HAVE BEEN ACCEPTED UNLESS THE PACKAGE IS RETURNED IMMEDIATELY TO US BY REGISTERED POST. THE ABOVE LISTED TRANSPARENCIES RECEIVED AND CONDITIONS AGREED.

Signed..

Photographer's contract

This agreement dated _____ between the above hereinafter called the Agency, and the Photographer _____.

1. The Photographer agrees that the Agency will be his sole selling agent for the sale of reproduction rights in those stock colour transparencies (and no others) supplied to the Agency and duplicates thereof in all countries for all uses and without sales restrictions except those advised at the time the photographs are supplied. It is also agreed that similar photographs will not be submitted to any other agency.

2. The Photographer agrees to the Agency taking a sales commission of 50% on monies received from all sales.

3. The Photographer warrants that all photographs placed with the Agency are his own exclusive property and copyright and that a model release is available unless stated to the contrary on the photograph or mount.

4. In the event of any claims whatsoever being made against the Agency from the subject matter of the Photographer's photographs subsequent to the Agency's offering them in the ordinary course of business on the Photographer's behalf, the Photographer will indemnify the Agency fully against any such claims.

5. The Agency agrees to send the Photographer an advice of sales made within one month of payment of their client's invoice, listing the transparency, size, rights sold, and media.

6. The Photographer agrees that all his photographs sent to the Agency will be retained for a minimum period of five years, and also agrees that a minimum of three months notice of intention to withdraw his transparencies.

7. The Photographer understands that whilst every care is taken with transparencies, in common with most other agencies, FOTOBANK cannot accept any financial responsibility whatsoever for photographs left in their possession by the Photographer or left or delivered to any of its clients.

The above conditions understood; agreed, signed:_____ for the Photographer.

Date:_____

Agreed, signed:_____ for Fotobank.

Date:_____

Appendix 2

The Fotobank Computer System

In any picture library, one of the most difficult areas is cross-referencing, retrieving, and sending out pictures; keeping track of them, making sure that they are returned, and invoicing the client; and making sure that once they are returned, they are filed in the right place so that they can be found for the next client. It is also very important to make sure that the client receives only those pictures which really meet his requirements; sending the wrong pictures is wasteful, inefficient, can alienate the client, and means that they are not available for other use. The computer is a natural candidate for this kind of demanding and meticulous work, and there are various computerised systems which can be applied. Ideally, though, the program should be custom-built for picture library use, and at Fotobank International Colour Library, we use one of the most sophisticated computer systems in the world. It is a fully integrated system, which is divided into a number of modules: FOTOBANK PICTURE CONTROL, DESPATCH, MAILING, ACCOUNTS, JOB SHEET, PICTURE SOURCE and PICTURE TRAFFIC CONTROL.

FOTOBANK PICTURE CONTROL is the basic picture library module. It is used for picture cataloguing, cross-referencing, picture search, and (with auxiliary video disc) picture display.

Pictures are catalogued by photographer, by country, by category, and by subject. As each batch of photographs is received, it is logged on the computer; as this is done, the label (with caption) is also automatically produced, and the basic information for cross-referencing is inserted. This is done with the help of keywords, which are user-defined: for example, a picture might be captioned *USA/California: Redondo beach, sunset*, and any of these headings (USA or CALIFORNIA or REDONDO or BEACH or SUNSET) could be defined as a keyword for searching. If it were a picture of a couple walking hand in hand, silhouetted against the sunset, it might also be cross-referenced under COUPLES and even SILHOUETTES. This is a rather extreme example – few pictures would be cross-referenced seven ways like this – but it shows what can be done. In fact, even more cross-references could be added, such as adding the suffix -TYP to BEACH; this would be used to indicate that it was a typical beach scene, not necessarily tied to any one location, which could be used for any purpose requiring an absolutely typical beach scene. Other suffixes include CAL (for Calendar), FC (for Front Cover), MOOD, and so forth: the individual library defines these, just like the other keywords. It is also possible to note whether the picture is horizontal (LS for Landscape format) or vertical (UP for Upright).

Although the program itself is extremely clearly structured, it also allows the maximum possible scope for the user to tailor it to his own requirements: for example, the "category" section is entirely user-defined, and there is a space for an "owner number" which allows you to key in the computerised system to your old manual (or electronic) system. The pictures are normally physically filed under the category in which they sell best, though they can equally well be filed under accession number; filing them in categories makes life easier for those clients who prefer to come to the library in person, and look through as large a selection of pictures as possible.

The way in which the picture search works will by now be obvious. Any keyword *or combination of keywords* can be selected, and the computer will run through all the information on all the images stored in the data bank, and then display the picture number together with other basic information, so that the pictures can be physically retrieved and viewed – or, with the optional (but rather expensive!) videodisc system, viewed on a screen.

Many libraries are rather daunted by the prospect of putting all their pictures on to the computer, but it need not be anything like as difficult as it seems. Most libraries know that ninety per cent of their income comes from about ten per cent of their pictures, and which subjects sell best – for example, at Fotobank International we always have plenty of requests for London subjects – so these are the ones to enter first. It is not always easy to identify all of these strongly selling pictures, but many of them can be chosen from memory, and the remainder can be identified almost automatically by logging in pictures as they are returned from clients: the pictures which go out are (almost by definition) the ones which sell best, and so logging them into the computer can be relatively painless. Of course, there may be new categories or special subjects which you particularly want to promote, so you can enter these as they are received, or during a lull in your frantic sales.

DESPATCH is, as its name suggests, used for controlling the despatch of pictures to clients – but it also does far more than that. Picture details are automatically printed out on the delivery note (with pre-printed terms and conditions), and if the client has not made his selection and returned the pictures within 28 days, a reminder is automatically sent out: this informs him that the pictures are now overdue, and that a holding fee is payable. If after two calendar months there is still no response, a second reminder is automatically produced together with an invoice for the holding fee – though for some clients, you may wish to suppress the holding fee invoice and just send them the letter, which is also possible. The fee is a fixed amount per transparency per week, and is set high enough to encourage return of the pictures, but not so high that it discourages repeat use of the library. If there is no response to the invoice, our policy at Fotobank is to turn the larger debts over to our collection agency: we always inform new clients of this policy when they first begin to deal with us, in order to avoid misunderstanding or unnecessary embarrassment.

MAILING enables the picture library to print out letters (or mailing labels) to clients, based on the type of business in which they are involved (advertising, travel, posters, book publishing, or whatever), their geographical location, or their previous known requirements (whether specialist or general). In any creative business, there is also a general tendency for businesses to be known by the names of their founders or owners, which can lead to some difficulties in addressing – Robert Harding the man might be catalogued under *Harding, Robert*, but his picture library might appear under either his first name or his second. MAILING allows either to be used, and removes the risk of duplicated mailings to *Harding, Robert* and *Robert Harding*.

ACCOUNTS is an accounts package specifically designed for picture libraries, who are in the position of having to pay photo-graphers as they sell their pictures, as well as having to invoice clients in the usual way. The program can handle both photographers who are registered for sales tax and those who are not, and provides them with monthly, quarterly, or half-yearly statements at the option of the library. All the usual features are also incorporated, such as client statements, debtor and creditor analysis, credit notes, and instant interrogation as well as regular end-of-month (or quarterly, or even weekly) reports. A particularly useful feature is the availability of sales analyses by category, photographer, subject, location, and time of year, which allows very detailed analysis of markets and of the sales success of the various photographers represented by the library, and can be extremely valuable in timing your various promotions and planning your general sales strategy.

JOB SHEET is an optional add-on package to the accounts program, which allows any item of expenditure to be allocated to a particular project, whether it is a shooting trip to New York, a few rolls of film, or an advertising promotion. At the end of the project, or at the end of the year, you can analyse the profitability of the various projects individually, which is obviously immensely valuable for cost and profitability control. Comparisons of job sheet expenses and marketing analyses allows the production of a really accurate budget forecast, and helps you to keep within the planned budget.

PICTURE SOURCE is extremely useful for inter-library deals, where a picture is not available from a library's own stocks but can be obtained from another library (or photographer, or other source) on a split commission basis, and can also be invaluable to picture users. The program consists of a basic list of several hundred general and specialist picture sources – picture libraries, individual photographers, museums, art galleries, government agencies, and major companies who maintain their own picture libraries. The user can then add his or her own list of sources, constantly updating the whole list as necessary, and adding optional personal appraisals of quality, range of subjects, speed, and cost on a "star rating" basis from zero to five. It is exceptionally useful to the individual picture researcher, as an infallible *aide-memoire*, but to a publisher or advertising agency or anyone else who maintains a picture research department, it is all but indispensable. Like the FOTOBANK PICTURE CONTROL package, it allows keyword random search – invaluable for those names you can't *quite* remember. This module can be run on its own, but it is even more versatile if it is run in conjunction with the next package.

PICTURE TRAFFIC CONTROL is a unique system for monitoring the pictures borrowed from different sources for different projects. Even on a single project, it is difficult enough working out who loaned what, and when it must be returned, and so forth; and when they are sent to third parties, such as designers or printers, it can become a nightmare. With more than one project, it requires very strict control indeed, which is made vastly easier by this package. Pictures are logged in as they arrive, and thereafter the program can be run daily, weekly, monthly, or on demand at any time, to see the precise status of your holdings. When you return the pictures, the system automatically produces a letter which details the pictures you are returning and the pictures you are retaining,

together with a brief "thank you" courtesy letter, which obviously saves a great deal of time and enhances your reputation for returning pictures safely and on time. If you send two copies of this note, one can be returned to you as an acknowledgement of receipt. If you do not want to list the transparencies individually, it is also quite possible to enter them as a batch; but unless you are returning *all* the pictures from a particular library, this obviously does not allow such close control. Once again, this package can be run on its own.

The entire Fotobank system can also be linked to other commercially available packages, such as word processing, Telex, and so forth. It was designed by a leading international photographic library, in consultation with picture researchers and publishers, and implemented by a leading software house; this obviously means that it is likely to be better suited to users' needs than other systems, which are usually designed by computer systems analysts rather than by a working library. It is not the only system on the market, but it is probably the best and certainly the most cost-effective.

INDEX